Cry for Me

A Novel

By Toni Mariani

Copyright Page

Reference Page

Butch Cassidy and the Sundance Kid, top grossing film of 1969 with proceeds of $103 million in the US alone

Theme song by Burt Bacharach

Miles Davis, Kind of Blue

John Coltrane, Giant Steps

Elvis Presley "Are you lonesome tonight"

True Grit, blockbuster film of 1969

Ben Hur, blockbuster film of 1969

Tyrone Davis, Can I change my mind? 1969

The Temptations, My Girl

The Temptations, Just my imagination, 1971

The Four Tops, Reach out (I'll be there) 1967

The Impressions, I'm so proud, 1967

Sam and Dave, Soul Man 1967

Chi-lites, Have you seen her? 1969

Friends of Distinction, Grazing in the Grass, 1969

Smokey Robinson, Ooh Baby Baby, 1965

David Ruffin, Walk away from Love, 1975

The Jackson's, Lovely One, 1980

Chante Moore, Chante's got a man

Keith Washington, Kissing You
https://youtu.be/KDa3eYevoHQ
Rumors,
https://youtube.be/1vwy5YcvMjU

George Benson, This Masquerade, 1976, https://youtu.be/cYYW6A3Q44U

 Harold Melvin and the Blue Notes, If you don't know me by now,

The Commodores, Sail On

The Commodores, Three times a Lady

Jesse Powell, You

Bobby Womack, If you think you're lonely now

The Dramatics, In the Rain

Dedication Page

    This book is dedicated to the friends from my neighborhood that I grew up playing with and walking to Sheridan Elementary School with. To their parents and grandparents who watched out for all the children in the neighborhood, and called to us when the street lights came on to get inside.

    It truly takes a village to raise children to be productive citizens, to help each of them stay away from illicit drugs and dangerous people and not end up in prison or dead. To the teachers of BJHS who helped us get through school there, and to enjoy our preteen years, and to progress to High School. And to the teachers of BHS, who helped in educating us and watching over us as we passed through your halls.

    Thank you.

    Toni

Table of Contents

Preface

It began with the father. Frank fell in love with a multiracial high school junior. He's Italian and his father was not having it. But neither was her father going to allow it, so they had to take their love undercover.

It happens again in the next generation, that lust for the darker berries of the sisterhood call woman. How far will this generation go to seek fulfillment for that which is forbidden to them?

The youngsters first meet in elementary school. Despite the odds of racism, parental strife, sibling rivalry, and a possible divorce their love grows from puppy infatuation to a deep abiding everlasting love. Their love wouldn't be denied and even a crippled mind will not stop it; or is that what happens in the fathers case? Read and find out.

Chapter One

"Girls, it's time to wake up and get ready for school!" Mrs. Hazelton called up the stairs loudly. "It's your first day there, and I know you don't want to be late."

"Ok mama," three of them answered. "We're coming."

Mrs. Hazelton wondered what the other two were doing since they did not respond. "Tawnie and Trina I didn't hear you respond!" she called out again. "Aslee, what are your sisters doing?"

"Mama Tawnie's already out of bed, so she must be in the bathroom, and can't hear you calling. I'll go see!" Aslee called out loudly.

"I think Trina's getting the clothes off the line that we forgot about last night," Raina called.

"As long as they're up and moving, leave them alone. Just make sure you three are moving. Time don't stand still you know!"

"Yes mama," three voices called out in harmony. The third voice belonged to the oldest sister, Aubree, who was the hardest to get moving. But since she responded, Mrs. Hazelton wasn't going to say anything else.

As their mother walked into the kitchen to check on their breakfast, and to turn the music back up on The Four Tops singing Reach out I'll be there, the three girls jumped out of bed and began looking for their socks and shoes. The usual objects that were missing when it came time to get ready for school, because they failed to prepare the night before. Mornings were a busy time for the Hazelton girls, especially during the school year. Since there were five of them, it took patience and love to get all of them out the door and down the street to school. This year would begin differently since it was their first day at a new school.

As Mrs. Hazelton stirred the scrambled eggs and flipped the bacon at the stove, she thought over the reason for their move into a new neighborhood over the summer. Two of the old neighborhood children had skipped school one day and were out running around when one of them dared the other to get underneath a semi-truck parked at a neighborhood grocery store. When the driver came out, he did not see the children playing around his truck and ran over the one who accepted the dare, crushing him. Even though her daughters just heard what happened, whoever relayed the information to them did so in such graphic detail two of them began having nightmares. Tawnie was now sensitive to even loud noises after the death of her friend. She could not stand any one to express outrage, could not tolerate violence, nor could she sleep through the night without at least once a week experiencing a nightmare. She began calling out the boys name, and end up screaming, reliving the trauma as if she had seen the entire event unfolding before her very eyes. Mr. Hazelton decided it was time to leave the area for good. He could not stand to hear his baby crying out in the night.

Mr. Hazelton was proud of all his girls; but Tawnie was his favorite, though he would cut out his tongue rather than admit it. He loved all his daughters, but she was just more in tune to what was going on around her, and would ask about his day and what was on his mind, just like a grown up. He sensed that she would be the one to take care of him in his old age. She was the musical child who wanted to take piano lessons, and play to his singing of the blues. He prayed that this school year in a new place and by meeting new friends, she would finally be able to replace the horrors of the telling of her friend's death, with new experiences. He hoped so because her cries in the night sent chills up and down his spine. As he kissed his wife while heading out the door to work, he told her, "See ya tonight sweets, and have a good day. I love you."

"And I love you Rollins. Be careful out there, see ya tonight."

"Bye daddy," chorused through the front door reaching him on the porch.

"Bye girls," he called to them.

Going back into the kitchen, Mrs. Hazelton asked, "Who needs help with hair this morning?" and then sat at the table while the girls ate.

"I can pull mine all back in one big ponytail and add a ribbon, mama, but thanks for the offer," Tawnie spoke up first.

"Mama, you know I need help!" the youngest Raina said loudly.

"Yes, I do know you need help, missy, but don't shout," Mrs. Hazelton corrected her.

"I can ask Aubree if she will help with mine. Aubree, will you help me with my braids?" Aslee asked her oldest sister turning to her.

"On two conditions," Aubree told her teasingly.

"What are they?" Aslee questioned.

"That you ask with a please, and that you pay me milk money for doing it," Aubree told her smiling.

"Ok. Aubree please will you help me, and yes I have an extra dime. How was that?" Aslee asked her.

"That's better. I'll start now, because we don't want to be late. Can you go get the comb and brush?"

"Mama, do you mind if I'm excused?" Aslee asked looking over at her mother.

"No, scoot scoot, and hurry back. No dilly dallying, you know how you are!" she said sternly to the second to the youngest, and the most talkative one, who drove her sisters crazy. Aslee was always been told to "hush, you talk too much!"

"So, girls how nervous are you to start school at Sheridan today? Are you worried about anything? I know you all will fit in and meet new people easily, you're so sweet and easy going," Mrs. Hazelton eagerly said.

"I think we all had time over the summer to meet some of the kids who go there, and since Tawnie and I played tennis on the playground, we know some from that end of the neighborhood," Aubree said with an upbeat and positive tone to her voice.

"Mama I feel nervous," Raina told her mom sadly.

"Well don't be, because I'm going to your class, and I will be there all day. Your teacher, Mrs. Norton asked me to be the room mother for the first week, so I'm taking the cookies we baked last night with the cheese balls and crackers. Are you glad Raina?"

"Oh, mama! I'm real glad!" Raina told her cheerfully. "Mama, can you make me one ponytail like Tawnie has?"

"Raina, you know your hair won't go into one yet. Her hair is longer and thicker than your hair, and even with your added ponytail piece, it won't look right because your hair is uneven. Maybe next year with proper brushing and care over the summer, your hair will grow, and you can have it in just one. For first grade you should have long pretty hair, but for kindergarten you have to have a lot of braids with barrettes. Okay?"

"Alright mama," Raina said with sadness in her voice.

"Trina did you get all the clothes off the line?" Mrs. Hazelton asked.

"Yes ma'am. I didn't get them all folded and put away. I took out what I had in there, but that's all."

"That's fine. When I leave school at 2:00, I'll rush home, start dinner, put that load away and start a new load. So, when you get home, change into your shorts and there will be a new load to hang out, okay? Then about 7:00 I want you to take them in. Whose week is it to do dishes?"

"This week is Aubree's turn. I'll sweep down the inside and outside stairs, finish any homework we get and then practice my lessons for the piano recital on Saturday. Did daddy say whether he has to work overtime mama?" Tawnie asked making sure her daddy would be there.

"I don't think he has to work this Saturday. He told me he made sure to take off, so he can take you to the recital. I will be there if I don't have to help bathe and dress Granny, but Saturday is my day to help with her. I'll come in late if I have to, okay?"

"That would be nice mama. Okay, I'm leaving now. I'll try to walk slowly but I want to catch the Anderson girl's as they leave their grandma's front porch," Tawnie called out as she jumped up and grabbed her backpack.

"We'll be right behind you," Mrs. Hazelton said, washing her hands. "Trina, is that what we picked out for you to wear? That skirt is very short. You must have grown since we bought it in the spring!" Mrs. Hazelton said amazed.

"I have mama. At the rate I'm growing, when I reach sixth grade I'll be tall as daddy!" she said disheartened.

"Lord I hope not. Your daddy is 6 feet 4 inches tall, sweetheart. No girl should get that tall. Well, I'll try and take it down or add a ruffle tonight, so when you wear it again you're not showing all your thighs. There is nothing a boy likes more than girls thighs."

"Mama I'm just in fourth grade!" Trina said nervously.

"I know darlin, but boys start looking in kindergarten!" Mrs. Hazelton said matter of factly.

"So mama, today boys are gonna look at my thighs?" Raina asked worriedly.

"If they do I'll be there to tell'em to put they eyes back in their heads!"

"Mama, what about next week when you ain't there?" Raina asked.

"Raina, use "are not", please. By then you will know how to tell'em, okay. So, don't start worrying now," she told the youngest child, who was a constant worrier.

"Aubree, there's the Marichelli boys. Will you have one of them in your class?" Trina asked her sister who would be in sixth grade.

"I think the tallest is Rico, and yes he's in sixth grade too. How do you know them already?" Aubree asked Trina.

"Saturday when we were on the playground shooting hoops, four boys showed up. When I asked Mary who they were, she said the Marichelli brothers. She said they are were an Italian family who lives not far from here and that they come over almost every day to shoot baskets on the basketball court."

"Well, girls, don't forget what I told you about boys. No matter what they look like, you are all beautiful young ladies and I don't want to have to beat no butts over my girls. Friendships are okay, but make sure they keep their hands to themselves, right!"

"Yes mama!" all four girls said at once. Tawnie was walking ahead of them with the Anderson children and didn't hear the conversation. As far as Mrs. Hazelton knew, she had no interest in boys at this stage in her young life. She was dedicated to her piano lessons for now. She prayed it stayed that way, because Tawnie was going to be a raging beauty when she grew up. All of her daughters were pretty to her, but she wasn't sure if she was just thinking from a mothers perspective or not, but she didn't think so. She had watched strange men watching all of her daughters and knew she was going to have a time of it as they grew older.

"Okay girls, we're here. Does everyone have their lunch boxes and milk money? I'll see you sometime throughout the day, but I am here for Raina, so don't count on it. Have a good day, be good and be polite to everyone. Love you all."

"Love you mama," they all chorused.

Mrs. Hazelton watched as her daughters turned down the hall to their individual classrooms. She was worried. With the talk of boys, and not just boys but good-looking boys with a fine ass daddy came problems. Yes, she had noticed the boys noticing her daughters. She was no fool. She had a tight grip on her girls and knew if she pulled any tighter the rope could break, and the closeness they shared might be harmed irreparably if she were not careful. The struggle was real, and more difficult trying to raise *five* daughters. Even with a two-parent household, there was no guarantee that they would be successful. She prayed a lot and left it in God's hands, knowing that with a three-fold cord in her marriage, prayer and love the family had the best chance to succeed. What she had not done, but what she thought she would do was bake a cake, take it to the Marichelli home, talk to the mother and find out what kind of moral compass she had. Sometimes with communication and friendship, a bond formed with another family that lasted and any problems that might have been do not appear.

After a few hours in Raina's classroom, Deidra Hazelton slipped out and walked home, checking out the new neighborhood. She saw plenty of space between houses, which to her was a sign that the adults were homeowners who had good paying jobs. That was a positive, which meant these were caring people, who probably attended a religious organization of one kind or another. She wanted her girls to play with god-fearing children, not those who were allowed to run the streets, with no home training and were being raised by mostly absent parents. The world's scene was changing, and sadly not for the better. The evidence was all around and could be seen by anyone who paid attention. The inner cities were full of drugs, gangs roaming the streets and that was one of the reasons her husband moved them from his home town. Everything was out in the open, no longer hidden behind closed doors. She did not want any of that around her girls and would do whatever was necessary to see that they had a happy and peaceful childhood.

∞∞∞∞∞

That evening, Deidra spoke to her husband Rollins about what she saw while walking home from the elementary school. He agreed with her about what it meant; that the neighbors here would be friendly and watch out for each other's children. He told her that he found the same on his job; good people who worked hard and went to a church. They loved that the community had a central play area and that she had seen plenty of parents outside watching their own children and others. That way if a mother was hanging laundry, preparing her families dinner, or had to run to the store there would be others to peek on the children and she planned on making sure they knew she could be counted on to do her share.

She started in baking the cake she planned on taking to the Marichelli's tomorrow and her oldest girls came and sat around the kitchen table to finish homework. She loved her new kitchen because there was a lot of cabinet space. The old place didn't have nearly this much room. As she stirred and mixed, the girls did homework, and they all listened to jazz. Music she found was not only a calming influence, it helped to stimulate the cells that would lead to performance and abilities and could help her daughters choose the arts later in life. She wanted them to be more than productive, but well educated, college graduates who were well-rounded and good wives for their husbands. In this, she knew that her example was critical, because children often mimicked what they saw. If her and her husband had disagreements, they took it into their bedroom away from the girls and she let her husband make the final decision, after he listened to her opinion. He was the head of their family, and she respected him to take care of them. He might have been the head but she was the heart and that was just as important.

After starting a load of laundry that someone would have to fold, she called the younger girls down to make sure they had prepared their clothes for the next day. She had them clean their shoes, prepare their hair decorations and find socks that matched. It helped to do this the night before because with so many girls in the family, a shared bathroom was hard on everyone. Maybe one day they could afford a house that had two or three. It seemed like she was always looking forward to one day, but that was what hopes were, some day in the future. As long as she kept living, she knew she would have her 'one day'.

Chapter Two

"Class, please welcome our newest student, Tawnie Hazelton!" Mrs. Richmond the fifth grade teacher called out.

"Welcome Tawnie!" all the students shouted at once.

"Tawnie, have you met any of the other students yet?" her teacher asked.

"Only Rachel, so far Mrs. Richmond."

"Okay, then Rachael I will ask that you show Tawnie around today. I saw you all here at the Back to School function, so I know you were able to walk around to some parts of the school, but to make sure she does not get lost, we'll let you stay with her for today. Okay girls?"

"Yes ma'am," both girls called out.

"Now, this year we will choose the classroom monitor/chalkboard washer in alphabetical order, so A's first. Amy, today will be your day. Bryen, tomorrow will be your day. If any student is ill or missing for a day, the person who lives closest to them will drop off any homework to them that same day after school. There will be no homework on the weekends. I think weekends should be for family, and a time to be stress free. If you have any troubles here or home, let me know privately and we will work together to find a solution. I will post everything we discuss each day on the bulletin board in the back of the room, so look back there if you forget. Okay let's get started. I'm so happy to see your smiling faces."

With that said, Tawnie began her day in her new fifth grade class in a new school and neighborhood. She was relieved to get out of the old neighborhood, because her family walked to school and every day they passed the spot where Jackson had been run over by the semi. She tried to get it out of her mind, but sometimes out of nowhere she thought of him and knew it was just her imagination, but she thought she heard him screaming out, and saw the expression on his face before he died. None of that was possible, because the body had been removed before the children were released from school that day. She knew she had a long way to go before she forgot Jackson, because he had been sweet and the class clown.

During lunch, Tawnie noticed one of the boys from her sister's class staring at her. It was the sixth grade Marichelli boy, Rico she though his name was. When she looked at him he winked, and she turned away surprised. He looked like a young Tryone Powers, her favorite actor after Gregory Peck, who she thought Bryen Marichelli looked like. She saw her sister Aubree and waved.

After school, Tawnie went to find her teacher. She wanted to invite her to her piano recital on Saturday. While backing out of the coat room, she bumped into someone. It was Bryen, the Marichelli boy in her class. She thought he was very handsome. His brother Rico was just as handsome, but in a different way. Bryen, she noticed had thick black hair that hung in a different way than Rico's wavy curls did. She couldn't decide who was cuter.

"Oops, scusa. Sorry, but I'm looking for my cello. Do you see it in there?" Bryen asked Tawnie.

"I think so. There behind the ball barrel. I've gotta run down to the music room. Excuse me," Tawnie said in a hurry.

"I'm going that way too. Wait and I'll show you the way." Bryen went into the coat room and grabbed his cello. With it in his hands he said quietly to Tawnie, " Andiamo. Let's go."

Bryen had noticed Tawnie the day the Hazeltons moved into the neighborhood. He was shooting hoops that day on the playground that sits in the middle of the neighborhood. All the children and adults played either basketball, baseball, played on the swings or sat on picnic tables or park benches. It was a nice gathering place in the summer or after school while it was still warm outside. That day Rico, Bryen and the other brothers were all shooting baskets trying to score the most points, and they saw the truck pull up and wondered who was moving to the neighborhood. When Bryen saw all those girls in one family, he wondered when the boys were going to get out of the truck. When the parents piled out, he knew there would be no brothers to follow. He watched the one who looked to be his age and liked the way her halter top showed her golden skin and the way her shorts rode up in the back. Her hair was up in a long, thick, black ponytail and she had a spiral on each side of her head, near each temple. She was gorgeous he thought. Different from all the other girls he knew. When Rico threw the basketball ball into his chest, Bryen knew that he'd better get his focus back into the game or he wouldn't hear the end of it. Rico thought that he was better at everything, just because he was two inches taller.

∞ ∞ ∞ ∞

That night after Rico and Bryen settled down in bed, they began talking over their day. Rico had seen Bryen only at lunch.

Rico who was an extrovert asked his brother, "So, what do you think of the new family? I noticed you checking out the one who ended up in your class, Tawnie, I think they call her?"

"She's in the after school music program too. She plays the piano. And just think I almost dropped out of cello last year. I think if I leave it at school, and see if I can get a cheap old one from the music store I'd be more likely to keep playing. I'm not dragging that thing back and forth to school every day this year."

"That's great Bry, but you got away from the question. What's Tawnie like?"

"Chi sa! I didn't know that was the question?"

"Okay Mr. Smart Mouth. Keep it to yourself. I'll make up my own mind."

"Rico, stay away from Tawnie. Yeah, okay, I like her! Davvero! So leave her alone. She's in my class. What about her sister, didn't she end up in your class?"

"Yeah, but she's not my type," Rico said snickering.

"So, you have a type now?"

"Go to sleep. You're not answering my questions, so I'm not answering yours!" he said stiffly.

"Avere una faccia da culo!" Bryen told him.

"Coglione!" Rico countered.

∞ ∞ ∞ ∞

The next day, after music class, Tawnie was on her way home, walking alone thinking about Saturday's recital when a car horn blew. She looked up to see Mrs. Marichelli driving with her boys from school. She leaned out the window and asked, "Ciao, hello, would you like to ride with us. We go by your house?"

"Sure," Tawnie told her, walking toward the car.

"How was practice and which instrument do you play?" Maria asked, turning down the radio playing Tyrone Davis singing 'Can I change my Mind'.

"Practice was good. I play piano," Tawnie told her getting into the front seat next to Bryen. "Saturday is the recital for all fourth through sixth graders in town. It'll be from two to four at the civic center downtown if you don't have anything else to do."

"That sounds like fun. I think Rico might have basketball practice, but the other boys and I will be there. They have a cousin from across town that plays piano and is in the recital. Tell your mom hello, and if I don't talk to you again before Saturday, I'll see you then."

"Sounds good, and thanks for the ride. See you later guys," Tawnie told the boys around the car as she got out.

"Say grazie, Tawnie. That's thank you," Bryen taught her.

"Grazie. Arrivederci!" Tawnie called laughing.

Bryen's eye popped he was so surprised. He hadn't taught her that.

"Nice girl, and pretty too. Black people sure do come in all colors," Mrs. Marichelli said to her boys.

"Yep, I noticed three shades in that family alone. Tawnie is golden, her sister Trina is a high-yellow, the lightest shade of them all, and the other girls are a richer chocolate like their father. Make that four shades, because Mrs. Hazelton is between Tawnie and the others. Why is that mom?" Rico asked from the back seat of their station wagon.

"From mixing the races. They probably have a great grandfather or mother from a European country, maybe even Italy."

"What, Tawnie could be part Italian?" Bryen piped up interestingly.

"Sure. Ask her where her people are from," Mrs. Marichelli told him.

"I will!" Rico said determinedly.

"No you won't! I will!" Bryen said sharply, turning to glare at Rico from the front seat.

"Bry, Rico! I know you two aren't already fighting over that girl! She might want a brown skinned boy. Did you ever think of that?"

"Mom, we're brown enough!" Rico said.

"I am any way!" Bryen spoke up. He was a shade darker than Rico and in the past thought that was a negative. But now he saw it as a positive and was determined to make it count as far as Tawnie was concerned.

"Fella's, I don't mind you having friends outside your race, you know that. But when it comes time to marry, your father will expect you to bring home someone who looks like us. And I bet Tawnie's father will expect the same thing of his children. I'm not being prejudiced, but there is a line. Now, hop out and get to your homework. I need to check the roast before your father get's home."

"Mom, after homework and before dinner I'm going down to shoot hoops. I need all the practice I can get before the game next week. I'll take Frankie and Lorenzo after I check their homework, okay?" Rico said expectedly.

"Sure, but make sure you have your watch on. Your father will expect all of you to be washed and ready for dinner at 6 sharp. Bry will you check Mario's homework and wash my car for me? Mario you help Bry, and then you two can go shoot hoops when you're done. Remember what we discussed. No fighting over a girl, blood is thicker than anything, right?"

"Yeah mom," her sons chorused back at her.

The door-bell rang and Maria went to answer it. She found a woman there who she thought might be the mother of Tawnie and her sisters. "Hello, come on in," she greeted the woman.

"Hi. I'm Deidra Hazelton. You may have seen my girls around the neighborhood or school."

"Yes, I have. I was just telling my sons that I needed to find your address and bring you a cake or pie. You were reading my mind. I'm Maria, come on in to the kitchen. While I start the dishes, you can cut me a piece of that delicious looking cake. Did you bake that?"

"I did. I used my mother's recipe. It's a seven-up cake, baked in a Bundt cake pan. I find that using her recipe makes the cake much richer than the others I've tried. I wanted to come meet you and discuss a few important points that I find interesting about the neighborhood. I walked home from the school yesterday and I noticed a few simple things like the playgrounds, the dense tree lines, and the space between the houses. To me all that combined makes for a good neighborhood, don't you think?"

"I do, and though I haven't expressed it that way I agree. Every day after the homework is completed the first place the boys head is down to the community playground. I don't worry about them coming to harm, just that their behavior might not be up to our families standards. You know boys, sibling rivalry, competition and posturing when it comes to girls. Do you see that in your daughters?"

"I can't say that I've seen any of that yet. It's still early though, they haven't come across any young men that they've been interested in. Except one young man who Tawnie had in her class. He was killed recently, run over by a semi at a market across from the old school they attended. Talking about a nightmare! Did you read about it in the paper?"

"I did and almost cried it was so shocking. I read that the one boy dared the other one to get under there. To live with that horror!" Maria said shaking her head.

"The parents must be grieving something awful. I have an idea. Let's take one of these cakes and something you'd like to bring, maybe coffee or tea and go visit both families. We can begin healing the rife that you know is going to come when the gossips get hold of the story. I know I would probably move out of the area if it happened to one of mine. Well look where we are today? We had no part in it and we moved away from there. Can you imagine being involved?"

"No! I think you have a great idea. We can look up the address and go tomorrow. I think a school day would be best, that way any children would not be involved. We want to speak with parents to get them to start the healing process and it will trickle down."

"Yes. I also wanted to know how you feel about mixed dating and marriages, because it seems that your sons are already looking at a few of my girls. Their dad and I don't mind, but I don't want it to come as a shock to you and your husband if it happens. Have you two noticed anything?"

"We did. In fact, we had to speak to two of them about competing for one of yours. I think my sons should know better, but feelings, emotions; the heart is not something that you can order to behave in a certain way. Right?" Maria asked Deidra.

"I agree. Emotions have no color, no culture, knows no prejudice and can hardly be controlled, so in trying to raise children we need all the help and resources available to us, and that is why I stay in prayer. I don't know what my husband does, but I stay in it because I don't think any of us can raise our children without God's help," Deidra told her.

"I've heard that new expression 'it takes a village' and I believe it."

"I've seen it! In the schools every day, that teacher could not teach such a large class if she did not have the help of a teacher's assistant and the help from parents that come and sit with small groups each week," Deidra told Maria.

"You're right, and I have my turn next week. Let me write down my phone number so that if you see something that we need to know about the boys, we can nip it in the bud early before it becomes a large mess. I think I will start praying more often, never really thinking about prayer outside the church day. I'm so glad you came over today, and I'll get started thinking what my gift will be to the families. Will you call me when you start getting ready so I'll be on time?"

"I will, and thanks for taking the time to visit with me and for your hospitality. It's refreshing to meet you. I'll call tomorrow, bye."

Chapter Three

Down at the community playground, while shooting hoops Rico saw Tawnie and all her sisters pushing each other on the swings. He went over and said, "Ciao, mi chiamo Rico. Hi, I'm Rico and those are my brothers Lorenzo and Frankie on the slide. Welcome to the neighborhood. Aubree and Tawnie I know, so can I get the rest of your names?" he asked while staring at Tawnie.

Since he was looking at her, Tawnie spoke up for them saying, "That's Aslee, Trina and Raina. It looks like all of you have one of us in the same class. How's the ball practice going?"

"Good. Why don't you and your sisters come and play against me so I can practice the moves I'll use against the other team?"

"Aubree is that okay with you?" Tawnie made sure it wouldn't just be herself alone. She wasn't sure why Rico was always staring at her, but she didn't want to ask either. She kind of liked the attention.

"Yea, let's go stomp this boy real quick!" Aubree said while laughing.

"Alright, let's go you three," Tawnie said pointing at the three younger sisters. About thirty minutes later Tawnie saw Bryen out of the corner of her eye. Since it was still the end of August, the girls wore shorts, halter tops and tennis shoes. When Tawnie would go in for the lay-up, Rico would find a way to touch her, and Bryen starting getting angry. He stepped up on the court and said, "Tawnie, come out now and let me cover your position. I think I heard your mom call you anyway."

She looked between the two brothers and said, "Ok Bry, thanks. Rico see ya later. Addio," Tawnie called waving.

"Yeah, buona sera, see ya later. We're walking to school tomorrow, so we'll pass by about 8:25. I'll whistle and you girls come out and walk with us," Rico told her.

"Okay Rico."

The next day Tawnie heard a whistle, and looked out the living room window. There, standing under the tree in her yard were all the Marichelli's waiting on the Hazelton girls. "Ciao everyone!" They all exchanged greetings. When Tawnie got a good look at Bryen's face she saw that he had a black eye. "Oh Bry! What happened? I'll be right back," she said as she ran back into the house. When she came out she had an icepack and put it on Bryen's eye and said, "Now hold that on at least until we get to school, then I'll take the towel back and put it in my locker. What happened?"

"The game got a little rough after you went in," Bryen told her. "But I'm okay."

"I'm glad Bry. I hate to think of you being in pain, because it looks sore. Did Rico tell you he was sorry?"

"No. But I'm not sorry about what I did to him, so we're even," Bryen said angrily.

"Bryen! That's not right. He's your brother and nothing should cause you two to hurt each other when playing a game."

"Tawnie, we're boys and we're going to fight. It's just a part of our makeup, so don't worry," he told her while reaching out to hold her hand. "Give me your hand. I'm okay. Why are you so sensitive?"

"I had a friend killed not long ago, and I can't stand any kind of violence. Please Bry, be careful. You could have been really hurt," she told him with tears forming in her eyes."

"Ah Tawnie don't. I promise you I won't intentionally get myself hurt again. Look, we're at school, and I know you don't want everyone to see you crying. They'll think it's over me, and then what will you do? Mi scusi, I'm sorry about your friend, but I'm glad it brought you here." Tawnie and Bryen looked each other in the eyes, and though they were too young to know about adult things, they knew that something was beginning for them that would always be there.

Rico watched and listened, and thought about his next step to get Tawnie to notice him. Since he found out that she played the piano, he thought it would be good to take up an instrument.

After school, on the way into the music room Tawnie ran into Rico and reacted in surprise asking, "What are you still doing here? Did you take up music lessons?"

"As a matter of fact I'm about to. What instrument would you choose other than piano if you could?"

"The saxophone. Have a seat and after my practice session I'll play you a tape, and you can hear what it sounds like."

"Okay, grazie tante. Thanks a lot."

Bryen walked in, saw Rico, knew what was going on and tried to ignore him, because he didn't want to upset Tawnie. He thought about her recital, and wanted her to have a good practice without drama from him and Rico.

After band practice, Bryen went up to Tawnie and asked her, "So what is Rico doing here? Did he say anything to you?"

"He told me he's thinking of taking music lessons and asked which instrument I thought he should start with. That's all, why? Didn't you know he wanted to try an instrument?"

"No!" Bryen said disgustingly, "and he never wanted to before you came here. He told me once I was a sissy for playing the cello. Now he wants to hang around the music room? Something's up, and I'm gonna find out what," Bryen said sounding angry.

"Bry, please, don't. For my sake, please? Let it go. Maybe it's real. Let's give him a chance."

"Tawnie, I know my brother. He's not interested in music, but I won't say anything yet. Let's see how far he goes, but if he does anything, says anything, touches you, let me know."

"I will Bry. Thank you." Tawnie left Bryen's side and went to his seated brother. "Rico, when you have time listen to John Coltrane and see if you like the sound of the saxophone. He does a beautiful job in the song "My Favorite Things". Then get Miles Davis' album from the music teacher and listen to him play trumpet.

That way you can hear the different sounds that each instrument makes, and decide what you would like to try out for several weeks. You can always switch between the two. On Saturday at the recital, all the musicians will join together and play a medley of big band tunes, so you should try and make it for the finale."

Bryen stepped up and added, "But we'll understand if basketball practice keeps you away. I remember what you said about music and how you compared musicians to sportsmen."

Rico ignored Bryen and looked at Tawnie while saying, "Thanks for the invitation Tawnie, and I'll be there. See ya in the morning. Bry, andiamo let's go!" he snarled at the end.

"Tawnie are you walking home alone?" Bryen asked her, concerned.

"No. Rachel's on the tennis courts. I'm going over to get her and we're walking together."

"Rico! Go on and tell mom I'm walking Tawnie and Rachel home first." Bryen called across the room.

As Tawnie and Bryen walked to meet with Rachel, they talked about their futures and life in general. Tawnie asked him, "Bry, what do you want to do with your cello, make it into a career?"

"Not really. I almost gave it up last year. I think I want to pursue my football, maybe try for a scholarship to one of the major universities and then go pro. What about you, how far are you planning on taking the piano?"

"I want to go as far as I can. Maybe get a scholarship to Juilliard one day."

"Juilliard? Wow, I would have to try for one of the New York colleges then, if I want to attend a school near you."

"If I don't get in I'll stay near home and go to the university in this state. Would you do the same?"

"Yeah. I already know I want to be where you are. We can talk about it more before it's time to go, but I wanted to see where your head's at, and see if I could fit in to your plans."

"Good idea because before we know it, we'll be in high school, and a few years later it'll be time to head to college. If we continue getting good grades and do well with our extracurricular activities we should be able to have our pick of colleges."

"It will take scholarships for me because with six boys to put through school, pops won't be able to pay for all of us to attend the schools of our choice unless we get extra help. I want to do well and help all I can."

"It's a little early to stress over it now Bry. I can already tell you're a worrier just like my baby sister. Let's take one day at a time, keeping our goals in mind but enjoying today is our priority, right?"

"Right! I gotta go. See ya in the morning. Oh, write down your home phone number on my notebook. Can you get calls from me?"

"Well, if mama or daddy pick up, say you have an English question, but don't say math, they know I'm terrible at it."

"Ok. It might not be tonight, but I want it in case I get a minute alone. Arrivederci you two," Bryen said smiling to the girls.

"Bye Bryen," Rachel, Tawnie's friend called.

"Arrivederci Bry, see ya in the morning," Tawnie whispered standing closer to him.

He stopped, turned back to her and winked. She wondered how this young Italian boy could be so smooth and cool.

Chapter Four

On Saturday, after the big band medley, and all the students received their applause, Tawnie came on stage alone and played a piece from "Butch Cassidy and the Sundance Kid" to a standing ovation. No one clapped louder than Rico and Bryen. They both shouted, "Brava, Tawnie, Brava!" Mrs. Marichelli noticed too and became worried. She knew it was time to talk to her husband.

That night, in the Marichelli dining room, with all the boys at the dinner table Mr. Marichelli began the conversation on race. "Boys, your mother wanted me to bring up a subject that we didn't think would ever have to be discussed here. But, we should have known better. You know we are not prejudiced against any race, but if truth be told we want you boys to have girlfriends of our race and culture, if possible. Italian Catholic girls would be our choice for you boys. Do you have any problems with that simple request, Frankie? Let's start with you. Are there any girls in kindergarten that you like right now?"

"I like all the girls, but I especially like Raina. I don't know if she is Italian Catholic though."

Oh Lord, Mr. Marichelli thought. We're in trouble now. He looked at his wife and widened his eyes, knowing what was coming. She shook her head, understanding too.

She asked the next child, "Lorenzo, is there a special girl in first grade that you like?"

"I like most of them, but they don't play with the boys. I like Aslee's color and her hair. She calls me Zo and I like that too. Dad is that bad?"

"No son, cause Jesus said love all people. We just thought you might find an Italian girl you can like as a special friend when you grow up. You can like all the girls and especially Aslee, if you want to. Mario, what about you son?"

"I like a girl named Christy, so don't worry about me. She's white."

"Mario. Honey, we didn't mean to make you think . . ." She shut up, because she realized she *did mean to* make him want a girl that looked like her. "Okay honey. Bring her over sometime."

"Sure mom," Mario agreed.

"Simon, can we skip to you? In eighth grade are there any pretty girls?" Mr. Marichelli asked quietly, worried what his son would say.

"Their all pretty. I like'em all, but no certain one, yet." Simon answered.

"Rico, how about you, son?" Mr. Marichelli asked.

"I like a few, but I want Tawnie!" he almost shouted in Bryen's face.

"She's mine, so forget that!" Bryen threatened.

"Boys, wait a minute!" Mr. Marichelli said. "Che cos'e questo? What is this? Why do you insist on making everything a competition? You're young and you two are brothers. There's plenty of time to choose a forever partner. Now is the time to concentrate on your school books, and work together in whatever sports you like playing. Bryen aren't you on the Knockers football team, and Rico you love basketball. Is that still where your focus is?"

"I'm playing basketball, yes. But, now I'm also considering an instrument. I think I want to take up the sax, or trumpet. I have to check out a couple more albums from the library before I know for sure. Chi sa!"

"The only reason he's talking about music is because Tawnie, my girlfriend is a piano player. He just wants to follow her around. I want you to tell him to leave us alone. She likes me not him," Bryen said glaring at Rico.

"I don't care who she likes. That will change anyway." Rico said menacingly.

"Rico, what do you mean?" his father asked him.

"Like you said pops, we're young yet. For now Tawnie might think she likes Bryen, but as she gets older, I'm sure she'll change her mind." Rico said matter-of-factly.

"Rico, if your mother and I asked you to let Bryen and Tawnie alone for now, and like you said, she'll probably grow out of this puppy love with Bryen, would you do it?"

"Sure! I just wanna try playing an instrument. I won't bother the finocchio and his girl." Rico snarled.

"Rico, that is uncalled for. Tell your brother you're sorry or face being grounded for a week!" Mrs. Marichelli stated firmly.

Rico quickly thought over whether or not there was an advantage to apologizing. He remembered that if he didn't and he was grounded he wouldn't get to see Tawnie in music class, because his mother would make him skip after school activities. He knew he better or else Bryen would entrench himself more deeply in her life. "Scusi Bryen. I didn't mean it, really." He quickly winked at Bryen.

Bryen knew just as surely as if he had heard Rico's thoughts out loud that Rico was lying. He knew that Rico planned to get in his way and try and turn Tawnie's attention to himself. Bryen would play along. "Grazi ," he answered Rico.

"Good, now what we wanted to make sure you guys understood is our position on mixed race marriages. Times are changing and as Catholics we try and love everyone. And not just in front of people, but behind closed doors and in our everyday life too. I haven't met any of Tawnie's family, although I see her uncle's playing basketball on occasion. Their good people, I know. What I won't put up with is division between you guys. I didn't have you to hear fighting every day, but to get along and be each other's friends before you have friends outside. If I find out you two are continuing this fight outside this house, you'll spend the whole school year with no extra activities except mowing the lawn here, and the lawns of everybody we know. For free! And in the winter, shoveling snow. Do I make myself clear," Mr. Marichelli asked looking between Rico and Bryen.

"Yeah pops," Rico murmured looking away.

"Yes sir," Bryen agreed looking his father in the eyes. Mr. Marichelli believed Bryen, but he didn't believe that Rico meant anything coming out of his mouth. He knew that he meant to do just what he had been doing and that's exactly what he wanted to do, and Bryen with the softer heart would try to cover things up and keep the peace, but end up getting the short end of the stick. Mr.

Marichelli winked at his wife and nodded toward the upstairs. She got the message and said, "If you boys are done with homework, could you please rinse and stack the dishes and I'll do them later?"

In their bedroom, Maria and Francisco Marichelli hugged and began undressing each other. Weekends, after a game of golf and a few beers with friends was their time to be together. With six boys to teach and train, a job to attend every weekday, Big Frank as he was called liked to relax on the weekends. Being Catholic, Sundays were church and mass, but Saturdays and Sunday evenings were for him and Maria. He held her close to his chest, kissing her eyes, cheeks and lips. He especially liked her bottom lip because he thought it was full and pouty, like a Negro's. Like one special Negro; a girl from his past that he still regretted that he could not marry, or even date openly. In those days it was not done. Well, it wasn't done in his family at least. When his dad found out he was in love with a black girl he took Frank out and beat him half to death, which was the second time he had raised his fist to Frank over his choice of a lover.

"Are you out of your mind bringing that nigga here?" his father yelled while whacking him with a 2x4 board. "Stick to your own kind, ya hear me?" Crack, the board hit Franks back. His father had been drinking because it was a Saturday night, and it was his ritual. Tonight he drank and beat his family, and tomorrow he would hustle them all off to mass, as if nothing happened. Frank had gone and returned from the dance with his new friend Carmen. Earlier he had introduced her to his father and mother and then returned to find his father enraged.

Frank was in eleventh grade and wanted to take Carmen to the school dance, but he took her to meet his father and mother first. After the introduction his father asked to speak to him privately and told him, "Get that nigga outa here. Who told you to date a nigga? Can't ya find any of your own kind to date?"

"Non capisco Pop! I like Carmen for who she is, not for anything else. It's immaterial to me what color she is. She's kind, patient, and loyal to me, and those are qualities that I find attractive. Don't you? Isn't that what we're taught at church every Sunday? Or is it just talk?"

"Silenzio! Don't you raise your voice to me! This is my house, and if you don't like my rules, you know where the door is!"

"Pop, I'm taking Carmen to the dance not marrying her, although that doesn't sound bad either."

"Out! Get out!" his father yelled.

That night after the dance Frank took Carmen home, and kissed her goodnight, and went home. His father was waiting for him and after hitting him with the board, Frank left and wandered the streets walking and thinking. He couldn't believe the two sides of his father's mouth. One side said to love everyone, and the other called Carmen and other people like her names. After wandering through the park, he knew he wanted to be close to her again. He walked over to her house, and tossed a rock up to her window. She came to the window, and he called up, "My dad has lost his mind.   Well he's drunk, can you let me in?" She opened the window and he climbed up the balcony rails and into her bedroom. The whole room smelled like her, jasmine and vanilla. It was so warm in here, so comforting and feminine just like Carmen.

"Frank, are you okay? It looks like he hit you in the eye. Sit here on my bed while I get an icepack. Take off your jacket, tie and shoes and put them on the chair. I'll be right back. The albums are over there and the record player is under the table. Put something slow on," Carmen whispered.

Frank was thrilled. He'd always wondered what her room looked like. He'd wanted to get closer to her since ninth grade, but no matter what he did, she paid no attention to him. This year over the summer, he'd put himself in front of her father, Mr. McGary, asking to get the contract to mow their lawn and wash his car for funds for school. It worked. She couldn't miss him and it was all set up by her old man. He undressed and used her robe to cover himself. When she came back in, he took the ice pack and handed her his shirt, showing her the blood, and asking, "Carmen, per favore, do you think this will come out? I rented the whole outfit for the party and I have to return it Monday after school."

"I'll let it sit in hydrogen peroxide. That should do it. Turn out that light, and turn the colored bulbs on. Be right back." She stepped into her bathroom that was connected to her bedroom and Frank could hear her preparing his shirt. He put on Elvis Presley's "Are You Lonesome Tonight?"

"Frank, how's the eye, better?" Carmen whispered in her soft sensual voice. Music to Franks battered ears and ego. "We better keep it down cause mom and dad just got in bed. They were waiting up for me. What happened when you got home?"

"My pops was waiting up too, except he was drunker than when you met him. It seems he's a racist. Well, who knows if that's a true word for what he is;

maybe he's okay with black people at a distance but he doesn't want any in the family, let's put it like that. How are you, Carmen? I take it you had a good time tonight?"

"I did, and thanks again for taking me Frank. If I had known the trouble . . ." Carmen began mournfully.

"Shhh, hush that now. Prego! It's nothing. My old man is a drunk, and likes to beat up on the family on Saturday nights. He just needed a reason to start tonight, that's all." He pulled Carmen onto his lap while still sitting on her bed, turned her head to face him and looked in her honey colored eyes, stroked her cheeks and tapped her bottom lip with his pointer finger. He rubbed around the outer edges, and she opened her mouth to say something more, but he stuck the tip in and gathered some of her moisture and rubbed it around the outer edges again. Back and forth he played with her plump bottom appendage and finally included the top lip too. He tapped again, she opened and he leaned into her, holding her close to him and kissing and licking her mouth. He stuck his tongue in and she sucked and licked his mouth. Then she raised her hands to his hair and ran her hands through it, loving the feel of its silky thickness. While The Impressions, I'm so proud played on the stereo, they both began to moan and Frank's cock lengthened and stretched, growing until it begged to stand up and salute. Frank lay back on her bed, pulling her down across his body, and she felt and saw all of him, since he had stripped. Their fervor increased and the heat between them was almost enough to catch the sheets on fire. She kissed down his chest, circling his nipples with her tongue, suckling on them, and eased herself down his body. When she reached his manhood, she took his sack in one hand and began pulling on his cock length with the other, letting it flip around her hand over and over. Frank loved every minute, and asked her, "Carmen is your door locked?"

"Yes, Frank," and got on her knees to remove her nightgown over her head. She was lovely to his eyes, all honey-brown, except for her areolas which were a toasted color. She pulled her ribbon from her hair and ran her hands through it, allowing it to flow around her neck and back. It was not one shade of brown, but a mixture of shades between gold and medium brown. Frank became even stiffer looking at her hovering between his thick thighs , wondering if she would let him go all the way tonight, this night their first night that he prayed would be the first of many.

"Carmen, sei cosi seducente. You are very seductive, do you know that?"

Carmen shook her head and sent her hair flying. She then turned her body around so that her feet were at Frank's head, and his feet were at her head. He began sucking her toes and licking her ankles and worked himself up her body.

She did likewise for him. She got up to his knees and he asked her, "Carmen, baby we should have talked before we started this, but are you on birth control yet?"

"Mama and I went to the doctor two weeks ago and the doctor recommended them for me, so yes I am," she whispered, not wanting to stop making Frank feel good. Men do not know that when they show a woman that they enjoy what she gives him with moans and gasps, it is a huge thrill and turn on for her, and at this moment Carmen was feeling that now, and was getting into her zone of pleasure giving. She went back to touching and licking him. He stretched and raised one knee, allowing her access.

"Oh baby, brava Carmen, that is wonderful. Tonight I need all of you. Sei un dono. This is going to be good, but later I want to sink my cock all the way in and out through your back. That feels so good. Sei incredibile, sei bellissima. Aww girl, take it in, that's right, gulp it. That's right, swallow that thang, girl. Open your throat, baby, take it in. Don't choke. Can you raise my balls and lick under there. Yes, ooh, you do that so good. Ummm, ahhhh. Yes, yes. You are so beautiful Carmen, sei sei bellissima, and so good to me. Glide your tongue around the head, that's right. Oh Carmen, faster baby, oooooh Carmen, girl I'm gonna cum all over you. Don't stop my lovely one, oh don't ever stop, its coming baby, its coming, Carmen, Carmen ahhhhhh!" He pumped his body several more times and shot cum all over her mouth and face, neck and chest. It had been awhile, so he had a buildup.

"Girl, who taught you that!? Sei stupenda!" Frank said in awe after catching his breath.

"No one. I asked a couple of girls at school what I should do if I didn't want to go all the way. They told me what to do, and how to handle a boy's penis. Was it okay for you Frank?"

"Baby, it was beautiful, you're a natural. Let's go bathe and when we come out I want to look at you, and give you something to remember."

Carmen led Frank into the bathroom and ran a hot bubble bath. He helped her in, grabbed a sponge and washed her all over. She lay back onto his chest, he reached around to her front, gliding the sponge around her breast, flicking her nipples and splashing water in her face. She giggled and flicked her water-tipped fingers in his face. He stroked her all over with one hand, and used the sponge with the other. He used his hands like an artist working the clay, sliding across her hips and thighs, finally working his hand around and dived into her sweetest treasures; her clit with its peeping turtle-like head bobbing in and out. Carmen moaned, trying to close her legs, it felt so good. Frank reached her luscious thighs, held them open wider and slipped his finger inside her as far as it would go, and worked another finger in reaching for that spot, but never stopping the battering of her clit.

"Carmen, I'm going to make you ready to cum and then turn you around to ride my cock, okay baby? That way when I enter you, your body will be lubed enough that the pain of breaking through your cherry won't hurt as much. You look so good laid out for me like that, all wet and shiny. Voglio fare l'amore con te. I want you so much, and I'm glad I'll be your first man. You feel so good to me, and I'm so happy to be here with you. I don't know what I would have done without you tonight. I could just stay here with you forever, per sempre baby. Does that feel real good?"

Carmen was beyond words. She was on fire, and felt something gnawing at her core, a hunger like never before down between her thighs, in her secret garden, as her mother called it. She knew Frank could stop her hunger, and she couldn't wait to be filled up with all of his thick staff. She mewled like a kitten, and reached her arms up over his head, behind her. She stretched and twisted her body, opening her legs and started to scream, but Frank anticipated her readiness, had the sponge squeezed out, put it in her mouth and turned her body. He opened her legs and slammed her hot pussy down on his bulging, over ready cock. He put his mouth around the other side of the sponge and bit down, keeping his own screams at bay, not wanting to bring her parents running. They rode each other, thrashing and pumping to completion. Carmen screamed over and over, but Frank held her in his arms, helping bring her over the edge into complete ecstasy, whispering Italian words of love into her ear.

While resting against each other, they stroked the others body. Carmen washed Frank's hair, and he washed hers. This was a pivotal moment for Frank, because he knew it would be in defiance of his parents to continue to see Carmen. He had picked her up from here for the party so he knew it was fine with her parents who he was. Some people did not see color, only character and that's how he wanted to live the rest of his life. He knew lust, had lusted before and found relief, but what he was feeling at this moment with Carmen was something so much more than lust. This was the most erotic night he'd ever experienced. The stuff he woke up to wet dreams about. He thought he might be in love with her because right now he was totally entranced.

Chapter Five

Maria had been waiting on Frank to do this to her all day. She thought of him every day, all day while he was at work. Maria tried during their love making to reach all of Frank, but for some reason she could tell that he held himself apart from her, that sometimes he was not there in the bed with her but far away in his own past; a past that did not include her. She had never asked about his sexual experiences because she was afraid of the answer, but knew by the way he took such care of her that he was an experienced lover. She wondered who it was that had received the pleasure of being initiated into love by Frank, and wish it had been herself.

Maria and Frank met in college. Maria was studying to be a nurse and Frank was almost done with his engineering degree. She would see him in a small café drinking coffee, not far from her dorm. He always looked so sad, always sat by himself studying his books. One day she took it upon herself to make the introductions. "Ciao, mi chiamo Maria, may I sit here? I'm here studying to become a nurse. I hope I'm not imposing?"

Frank looked at her and thought 'my Carmen has a bottom lip just like that. My god, how did I mess things up so badly? I miss her so much it hurts, but it's over, and I need to move on with my life', but said, "No, no imposition. I have a quiz later today and I need to brush up, but go ahead, sit. I'm Frank Marichelli, nice to meet you Maria."

"Nice to meet you Frank. Valerno, Maria Valerno. How are you?"

Frank could only stay a few minutes, but they both said that this café was usually where they could be found during the school week. After parting, Frank didn't think of her anymore until she popped up in his face. Maria made sure she saw him every day before class but it took his entire senior year before he took her out on a formal date. His degree was important to him, and he needed to prove to all the naysayers in his life that he could make something of himself. He had to stick to his books and graduate in the top of his class if possible. He didn't have time for extracurricular activities with Maria. He remembered the words Carmen's father used against him when they found out he wanted to marry Carmen.

Frank was put out of his home. After church on the Sunday that he and Carmen became sexually active, Frank and his father had a discussion that led to another verbal altercation. Mr. Marichelli told Frank to get out and never show his face around his home again. Frank went to Mr. McGary his boss and told him what had happened, and Mr. McGary at first welcomed Frank and offered the room over his garage to him. Frank moved in and for awhile he and Carmen just walked each other home, and sometimes did homework in Carmen's living room. But of course, young boys get horny and Frank began slipping into Carmen's window at night. Their passion burned hot, and they were not ready to deny it, but feed it. This continued through the end of their senior year in high school, until Carmen prepared to leave for college.

Frank wanted to attend the same University that Carmen attended, but Mr. McGary told Frank no. He told Frank that Carmen needed to concentrate on her education; that without her degree she would be just another black woman on welfare. He did not want Carmen to diverge from the plan that he and his wife had made for her since before she was born. Mr. McGary felt that Carmen could be held up as an example for their race and possibly enter politics after her graduation. Mr. McGary was from the south and his thinking was shaped by having lived there for his young life. Matriculation for Frank into his culture was not something that her father could agree to. He wanted a nice young black man for his Carmen because that was the way he had envisioned her life.

Carmen yelled at her parents the day the confrontation took place, saying, "That's the problem! It's not your life, but mine. Mine and Franks!" she stated exasperated with them both. "When I leave here I want to lead my own life. I can't continue to be put on your pedestal, the pedestal for the whole black race. Mama, daddy can't you understand that?"

Her mother sympathized with her, even going as far as agreeing with her but she couldn't stand against her husband. It just wasn't done, and she felt that once Carmen was gone she still had to live with the man. Mr. McGary told Carmen that if she defied him, he would cut off all funding for her education and Carmen would be on her own, and see how far she'd get with the lawn boy taking care of her then. Carmen gave in, knowing that she couldn't allow Frank to shoulder the responsibility for both of their educational expenses. Neither one of them would make it if that happened. She left for college, and could not tell Frank where she would be attending. Frank mourned for the rest of that school year without Carmen, eventually heading off to complete his own educational requirements to obtain his degree in engineering. For awhile, Frank returned home every weekend to try and find out where Carmen went and watch the house to see if she would return. For three years she never did.

Then, over the summer in 1955 Mrs. McGary died and Carmen came home. Frank did too, and found her. Frank showed up at the mortuary and asked first, and then begged Carmen to go away with him. He promised to take care of her. Of course she wanted to, saying, "Frank, sweetheart, you are almost finished with your degree. I can't get in the way of that, and I am almost done as well. My father is all I have left and I can't defy him at this stage, so please wait until I graduate and I will come home to you my love."

"Carmen I want you so much, so even though I think you are making a mistake I will wait, my darling girl." He kissed her and squeezed her to his chest, and said, "Come with me to the hotel. I want you so badly, I miss you."

"I miss you too, more than you'll ever know. I'll meet you tonight. Wait for me, "she told him passionately.

That night they made love like the first time, bathing each other and bringing each other complete fulfillment. Frank undressed her and said, "Carmen, it's been so long and I have longed for this night. I dream about you every night, and I can't take this separation much longer. Non posso vivere senza di te. I wake up with a stiff cock and use my hand to release the tension. That's no way to live, baby. So I want your promise that as soon as you graduate you will call my dorm and leave your number with the attendant and I will come get you," and then kissed her with such tenderness and sadness she wanted to weep.

"I promise, Frank, and believe me when I say it has been just as hard on me, wanting to call and ask you to come get me. I am one of a very small number up there at NYU and it's not been easy. But it's almost over and I can put up with it knowing that I have you to look forward to. Ti penso sempre, now make love to me Frank, please?" She massaged Frank's penis until it stood up between them and then stretched out on the bed and he put her legs over his shoulders and leaned in to suck her large areolas, nipping them making her cry out and writhe under him. He moved down her body kissing and licking her all the way, until he reached her pussy and then groaned at the sight of her pink lips buried in curls and leaned in and sniffed and then licked her dew. She called out for him saying, "Frank I need you, my love, sei tutto cio` di cui ho bisogno, I need you so bad, please take me . . ."and then he drove himself in up to the hilt, slamming in her tightness and they both screamed out each other's name.

Carmen closed her legs around his back and wrapped her arms around him, hanging onto him for dear life. He pummeled and slammed into her over and over again, as though he wanted to punish her pussy for staying away from his cock for so long. He was actually punishing her, and took his anger out on her body. With each thrust he became harder, more aroused and more primal, wanting to batter her pussy until she knew that she belonged to him alone. She knew it, and only wanted to stay right where she was forever. They rocked with each other, crying in frustration and anger at the situation, but loving each other still. "Carmen," Frank cried, "why have you stayed away so long. You know you are the only one in my life. Sei la mia vita! Sei il mio incantesimo. You are my enchantment. You know I love you, you are mine, mine, and this pussy is mine. Say it Carmen. I want to hear you say it."

"Frank, I am yours, this body is yours, and this pussy belongs to the cock that is buried deep within it. I've been so lonely for you, so hungry for you and your love. I love you Frank. Don't cry. I love only you. Amore ti amo, ti adoro!"

He filled her so completely, so proudly, so hungrily and she was happy. She told him, "Frank I want to have your baby. If I get pregnant, I'll keep it close to me forever. We'll love you always Frank, no matter what happens."

"And I will always love you, Carmen. I will look for you, and want you forever." He felt himself tense up, felt his body preparing to cum, to explode inside her and he slowed down and let it cum, and filled her with his seed. He wanted her pregnant too, and prayed that it was so. She dug her nails into his back just like a hungry cat, and he loved it. She cried out his name one final time, and clenched his cock with her tightness, falling from her precipice into total ecstasy.

After their bath, they held each other all night. Carmen cried several times, but Frank held her tightly murmuring sweet words that meant something only to her. In the morning, she had to say goodbye, because she had plans to meet her father for breakfast. Frank gave her the details to his dorm and told her what he expected. He kissed her deeply, and watched her walk away. That was the last time he saw her. After graduation she received a call from the mayor of Washington D.C., and he offered her a position as Assistant Mayor with the promise of his position when he retired in several years.

What Frank didn't know was that Carmen went back to school and several months later she began throwing up. She thought it was the flu, but after two month she realized that she had lost fifteen pounds. She went in to see the doctor who took a pregnancy test, and confirmed that she was indeed going to give birth in seven months.

Chapter Six

After Frank and Maria finished making love, Maria once again felt empty. She wondered if it was just her, or did Frank really leave most of himself out of the equation. Where was he mentally when he entered their bedroom? She needed to speak to someone. She couldn't mention it to Frank, he thought she enjoyed their love making sessions. After six births, maybe he didn't find her body attractive anymore. Maybe she needed to lose weight. She would go and talk to Bryen music's teacher; hearing good things about her, including that she had training in family therapy. Not that she thought that she and Frank were in long-term trouble, but if she could get an outside opinion without judgments, she would take any insightful tips offered. Through notes passed between the ladies and the boys, she promised to meet her after school today.

While the kids played tennis on the schools tennis courts, Maria found the music room from the sounds of music coming from it. Right now she heard Sam and Dave's Soul Man pouring out of the room. She knew it would be pointless to knock as loud as it was, so she just walked in. She saw a pretty golden skinned lady, with long brown hair hanging in curls down her back dancing in the middle of the room. She went over and waved to get her attention. "Oh, sorry, I have to burn off my calories somehow. How are you today, Mrs. Marichelli?"

"I'm wonderful. Nice to meet you Mrs. Ashford and thanks for staying late to see me. The boys are raving about you and their lessons, so I knew I had to meet you. I also heard that you have a degree in family therapy, so I wanted to ask for your opinion."

"Of course, let's sit down. I'll turn this down," Mrs. Ashford said heading for the stereo.

Mrs. Ashford said she came from Washington D.C., but had lived in the town years ago. She'd married the mayor of D.C., had a son who was a year older than Simon, was now divorced and had returned to sell off her parents home and possessions. While checking out the job market in the area, she'd received a call from the school inviting her to interview for the position of music teacher. She did, and was hired. Maria told her that she was not from there, but had met her husband and returned with him after graduation. She found herself pregnant a year after meeting him in college.

"How did you two meet?" Mrs. Ashford asked Maria.

"To tell you the truth, I followed him and learned his routine. Once I knew where he hung out, I put myself there. I waited to see if he was involved with someone, and when I saw how lonely he was, I knew that he was single. I have to admit, I think I fell harder for him than he did for me. I thought being Italian would give me a leg up, you know, having something in common there was a foundation, maybe we could make a connection. I have never admitted this to any one before, but the first time we made love he cried, and now that I think about it, I don't think he was crying over anything we did, or me. I now know that he was mourning the loss of someone else. It's taken me all these years, and now I have clarity just talking to you about it. Oh my God, my man has been in love with another woman all these years," Maria said, breaking down into tears. Mrs. Ashford went over, wrapped her arms around her and held her saying, "Maybe not. Maybe you are misinterpreting everything. You've had him for fourteen years, right? There's been no one else has there?"

"Not that I am aware of. He's home for dinner most nights at six. He takes the boys for sporting activities. But Carmen, can I call you Carmen?"

"Of course, Maria," Mrs. Ashford smiled.

"Carmen, he's there physically. I'm not so sure about the mental part of him."

"Why not try something new?"

"New. I don't know if I've ever had the old! Like what?"

"Like a costume, a wig and a bold attitude. Role-play honey. Be you, but a new more dominating you. Have you ever taken charge in the bedroom, been tied up or tied him up? You can try blindfold-sex; give him some in the backseat of your car, sex at the drive inn. Girl, you were bold enough when you followed him around and got him, so now do it to keep him."

Later, after discussing life around the Marichelli household, the ladies made plans to meet again.

∞∞∞∞∞

Bryen told his parents that Tawnie would be coming over to practice a duet that the music teacher assigned them for the next recital. He wanted her to stay for dinner and asked his mom to make her special spaghetti dinner. She agreed and not many days later Frank watched while Tawnie and Bryen made beautiful music together. Rico watched too and grew angrier. He had not decided on which instrument he favored yet, but was right there in the music room after school making his presence felt.

Frank watched the two of them practice and wondered which of his sons Tawnie was interested in. She reminded Frank of Carmen, who was never far from his thoughts. He wondered what she was doing right at this moment and whether or not he'd impregnated her. He hoped so; if he couldn't be with her at least his seed would be. Frank kept his eyes on Rico too, because Rico worried him. "Rico, why aren't you practicing basketball with the fellas? Aren't you as interested in getting that basketball scholarship as you were before?"

"Naw pops! I'm going to meet with Mrs. Ashford the music teacher in a few days and hear some music by both saxophone players and trumpet players. I like what John Coltrane can do with a sax, but I also like listening to Miles play that trumpet. What sound do you like best? Hey why don't you come too and help me choose?"

"Sure son. What day do you meet with her?"

"I'll let you know. She has to collect the music and will get back to me," Rico told his father.

"Ok, sure I'd be glad to go. Try and give me a days notice," Frank said.

Mrs. Ashford was indeed Frank's Carmen. As she sat in her after school music class, she thought about her son, Frank's son out on the tennis court right at this moment, probably playing with some of his own half-brothers. She knew that Frank was going to explode when he found out that she had kept his son from him for all of his first fourteen years, and she felt a tingle of fear, but she couldn't deal with that right now. She had to prepare her mind for the confrontation that she knew was coming when Rico appeared with his parents. She wanted to be assured that Rico was fully committed and knowledgeable about the instrument he would choose and that he had his parents support and approval. She noticed the rivalry between the brothers and Tawnie Hazelton and wondered if the parents knew. For now, being as young as they were it was not much of a problem but if it dragged into high school and beyond, it could be. As she waited, she thought over her life in D.C. and how that turned into a disaster.

Her relationship with the mayor began in order to cover up her pregnancy, and the guilt over not returning to Frank as promised ate at her conscious for years. She didn't want to return home to her father as a pregnant black woman, and hear all the negative stereotypes that would have poured out of his mouth. He could express the most derogatory terms for black women than any person of any color she had ever heard. She couldn't face him. And then when he died, she had his attorney settle the house and had him take over the cleaning and storing of all their possessions. Now she had to come face to face with her lies and deceptions and shuddered to think about the fallout.

As she was listening to Smokey Robinson and the Miracles sing Ooh Baby Baby and dusting the piano top she heard Rico say, "Mrs. Ashford, we're here. This is my father Frank Marichelli. My mother had to stay home and finish dinner preparations."

As she turned around, she saw Frank with his hand out to her and a smile on his still gorgeous face. When he saw who the teacher was he stepped back stunned and dropped his hand. Frank was shocked to see that the teacher who was teaching his sons music, was his long lost love Carmen. In a fraction of a second he took her all in, examining the changes in her face and body; that luscious body that he knew every trace of. A body that he had tasted with his tongue, traced with his fingers, had known and touched and brought cries of ecstasy from. Her body, the one he had called his own, and had hungered for, ached for like no other before or after. Mine, she is still mine he thought, and has known no other man in the true sense of the word; the sharing and giving of herself to another as she had done with me so many years ago. Those thoughts flashed through his mind in the time it took to bat an eye.

"Dad, did you hear me? I asked if you had met Mrs. Ashford before." Rico mumbled to his father, embarrassed. "She's trying to shake your hand."

"I'm sorry son. For a minute I thought she reminded me of someone I knew."

"Frank, it's me Carmen. I've come home." With those words Carmen tried to convey her feelings about what she had done, to ask forgiveness and let him know that she still belonged to him, still loved him and only him.

Frank wasn't buying it so easily. He had been tormented for years and was still angry, and Carmen could feel almost through osmosis all that he wanted to say. Frank had to hear what she had to say for herself, find out what excuse she thought would soothe and calm his frustrations with her.

"Carmen?" he whispered, wanting to hurt her for just a moment out of all the thousands that he spent craving for the sight of her. "I don't remember the girls name . . ."

"Stop it Frank. We will deal with us after we let Rico share his thoughts on what he wants to do instrumentally. Rico, have you decided between the two yet?"

"I think I will try the sax, since Tawnie suggested it first, and give it a fair shot and then if it doesn't work out . . ." he stopped talking and watched his dad stare into Mrs. Ashford's eyes. "Dad?"

"Son?" Frank asked, and finally broke eye contact with Carmen, looking questioningly at Rico. "I'm sorry Rico. I think we'll let you choose whatever you want for now. Like you said, give it a shot. Would you like to pick out some music to take home and practice with, and we'll go see about renting a sax. I'll be about twenty minutes behind you discussing all the details with Mrs. Ashford. If you want to, go check out who's on the tennis courts and I'll come find you?"

"Ok dad, and grazie!" Rico smiled, not suspecting what Frank was about to do. Rico picked out a piece of sheet music and left.

Frank grabbed Carmen's arm and dragged her into the cloak room. He grabbed her around the waist, pulled her into his arms roughly with one hand and grabbed her hair with the other. He smashed her mouth with his own, and began kissing her as if he wanted to eat her alive. He forced her to take his tongue in and they began battling each other's mouths in a desperate race to satiate the hunger. He reached for her breasts and squeezed her through her blouse, pulling apart the buttons and popping a few loose in his urgent desire to get at her. He had to feed the beast, his cock reached and stretched out for her pussy, wanting to bury itself inside and never come up. It knew what it wanted and reached out for the place between her exquisite thighs. They both moaned and Carmen turned to face the wall, lifting her skirt and pulling down her stockings. In his haste, Frank tore them from her body and tossed them away, and ripped away her panties and reached for her pussy, shoving his fingers in deep checking for her wetness and found her dripping. He prepared to rape her if he had to, but she seemed as excited for him as he was for her. He whispered in her ear, "Now whose pussy did you say this was all those years ago, and who's been in it since?" he grabbed her hair, bending her head back.

"Your's, solo tua. Tu sei l'unico per me," Carmen cried. "Frank, sono pazzo di te. I've missed you my love. Don't punish me, please. But testa di cazzo, Frank, por favore. Hard Frank."

Frank took his cock in his hand, pulling it and jammed it in Carmen from behind. He wanted the lubrication from her nether lips for what he was about to do. He pumped inside her pussy several times, pulled out, bent her farther over, moved her legs farther apart, and felt for her back hole. He put his cock to her hole and pushed with all his might, and Carmen unprepared screamed. She did not try to get away, but accepted the punishment that Frank was trying to mete out. Frank froze because the grip that her rectum had on his steel rod was a shock, and he had never felt such unmitigated pleasure before. When he was finally able to move, he slowly shifted himself deeper into her ass. Carmen moaned and backed up a step to help ease him closer so that he was seated deep inside. Neither one of them had ever experienced such rapture, such carnal delight, nor would they forget who it was that they'd shared it with. They both loved it and knew that this was just the beginning. It was pure pleasure and because Frank had immediately reacted to Carmen after seeing her, it did not take them long to reach and fall into that place of inestimable fulfillment. They both cried out in release. Frank leaned his body over Carmen's back, rested for a few minutes and she willingly let him rest.

After resting, Frank stood and helped Carmen straighten up because he knew that he'd probably hurt her. She told him, "I'll go get some towels and wash you off. Wait for me here," and went to the sink. While he waited, he thought over what he wanted to say to her. He knew how he said it was just as important because though he was heartsick, he was relieved that she had returned and it appeared as if she had plans on remaining. Adding that in to the equation, he was able to calm himself. Now, where was her husband?

∞∞∞∞∞

When Carmen finished wiping off Frank's cock, he adjusted himself into his pants and told her, "Where is your man?"

"Frank, I'm alone now. I left him and then he divorced me."

"When?" Frank wanted to know.

"I moved out six years ago, but the divorce came through three years ago. Frank, I know we need to talk, and I need to share something with you, but your family's waiting. If you don't want Maria down here, you need to get Rico and get home. I wrote my details down for you, but let Rico put it in his notebook because I'd hate Maria to find it and connect the dots," she said handing Frank a note with her phone number and the address to the old house.

"What dots? Why would Maria connect me to you?"

"Frank, it'll have to wait. I'll tell you when you can get away. I leave a key under the matt at the back door. My bedroom is in the same place, but park away from the house for now. Kiss me my love."

Frank enveloped her into his chest, and pulled her head back and grabbed her bottom lip with his teeth, nipped it and said, "I'll be by tonight. I've waited for ass this good all my life and I won't wait any longer," he whispered, cupping her sweet rear end and grinding his front into hers.

"I'll be ready for you, vita mio," Carmen purred into his ear.

Frank grabbed her hand and rubbed it across his crotch, smiled and walked out.

Chapter Seven

At dinner that night, Frank was absent mentally. Maria noticed and worried. In the past she noticed his mind wandering around bed time, but not this early in the evening. Unbeknownst to her, Frank was thinking about his hour spent with Carmen and how fast he could get back to where they left off. The boys were wondering why their father was so quiet so Bryen tried drawing him into the conversation. "Dad, how do you like our music teacher? She's nice, huh?"

"Si, yes she is son. How are you doing with your cello? Are you planning on going all the way with it?"

"I think so. Mrs. Ashford thinks I'm good enough, and she said I should make sure I get to all the recital's and concerts put on by the school, and volunteer to help with the chorus when they go away on trips. If I volunteer to help them set up music stands, all that volunteer work can go on my application to Juilliard."

"That sounds real good son. Let me know when the next event is planned and I'll see if I can be one of the parent volunteers. Rico, I heard about an album of John Coltrane's that I think you should hear. After we help clean up here, let's go check it out, okay? And Bry, are you practicing with Tawnie tonight?"

"I could if you don't mind. Let me call and find out."

"Maria, I'm going out for awhile. Do you need anything from the store?"

Maria thought she might try the tip that Mrs. Ashford had given her about role-playing and needed to pick up a few things, but she wanted to surprise Frank and would need to go shop alone. "I'll need to go out tomorrow and meet Mrs. Ashford for lunch, so I can get what I need then; but thanks love. See if they have the new Jackson 5 album, though."

Frank thought, what the hell did she just say about meeting Carmen? What is going on with my wife and my mistress? I better go find out from Carmen. "Fella's I'll be out putting air in the tires. Come out when you're ready," he called while heading out the door. Lord, how am I going to get rid of Rico, Frank thought. I'm going to have to see if Tawnie and her sister's can go listen to records with both boys if I want to go see Carmen. Damn! When the boys were in the car, Frank asked, "Boys, would it be possible if both of you went with the Hazelton girls to listen to the albums Rico might use to decide on his instrument? I'll go in and ask the parents with you, but I need to go and see about a project at the office for about two hours, okay?"

"Sure pops," both boys chorused.

After getting permission from the Hazelton's, Frank dropped the kids off at the music store and went to The McGary house; Carmen's childhood two-story home. The house went back on the market right when Carmen needed to get out of D.C., which she saw as a blessing. Frank parked a block away, not sure why he had too, but he'd find out tonight. He used the key, walked through the downstairs remembering his years here, and slipped into Carmen's bedroom. She was listening to the Chi-lites singing "Have you seen her?" and he could hear her singing along. As he passed through her room, he thought that song could be the theme to his relationship with her, but no more. Never again would he allow her to stray, leaving him tied up in knots.

He noticed that she had redecorated and all the pinks were gone, and it was a more grown up combination of greens now. She had a love seat and a rocker added which were new. Frank walked into the bathroom and Carmen was in her bathtub, which was filled with bubbles. She opened up her arms to him, and winked. "Ciao Frank! Lock the door, please. We have company, and I'll introduce you later."

"That sounds intriguing, but Carmen I don't have time for guessing games tonight, so let's be straightforward with each other and talk," he told her perturbed, as he undressed.

"Frank, remember the last time we made love before I went back to school, and we talked about getting pregnant?"

"Yes, I remember. And?" he questioned as sank into the hot bubble bath. It smelled of her, the same scent he remembered from high school.

"We did indeed get pregnant then. I returned to school and before I knew it I'd lost fifteen pounds, and so I went to the doctor and found out I was already two months along."

"You had my child fourteen years ago and I'm just now finding about it? Carmen how could you do that?"

"Because I was alone and graduating from college Frank. I did what I thought I had to do at the time."

"And what exactly was that Carmen?" he asked cupping her chin in his large hand and tilting her face up so that she could look directly in his cool ocean blue eyes. They were stormy now with the passion and anger he was feeling.

"Please don't be mad at me Frank. I'm here now and I brought our son home. At the time I was offered a job as Assistant Mayor of D.C. This part you're not going to like, but I did it to hide my pregnancy because I didn't feel I could return home pregnant. I seduced my boss, and made him think our child was his, but I pretended to have a chronic condition post labor that would keep me celibate. Frank, I have not made love with anyone before you today, since that first time with my ex fourteen years ago. That's the reason he divorced me; I couldn't be a wife in every sense of the word. I had promised you that I was yours and I meant that but please forgive me for that one time. Can you forgive me?"

"Carmen, I forgive you, because I can't ever walk in your shoes. I remember how your father was, his attitude regarding the "race" and I understand you wanted to stay away from his sharp tongue. Come here," he said as he gathered her in his arms. "When will I get to meet my son?"

"Tonight, if you want to. Guess who he attends classes with? Simon! How are we going to deal with that?"

"That reminds me. Maria told me tonight that she's meeting you for lunch. Since when have you and my wife become chummy?"

"Frank, you have to remember, I'm your children's teacher, and with them both favoring another one of my students, someone's parent had to get involved. I'm glad it's Maria because unless we are going to walk away from each other again, we've all got to be on the same page, come to terms with our past and keep moving forward for our children. We talked about your relationship too. She feels that you have not always been present, mentally anyway. Physically, she had no complaints. And she didn't try to excoriate your record as a good dad but was proud that in that area she could only say good things. Frank, women have a special kind of intuition when it comes to sniffing out a side piece, and she didn't feel you had one. So, before she sniffs me out, I think we should be honest with her about what we feel for each other, and that our feelings will never change."

"I agree. What did you tell her to do to get me to be more present?"

"I gave her a few tips to use to get your attention like role playing that included a costume. She was a nurse, so she could dress up as a waitress with a real short cocktail dress, or play the hooker with high heels and red lipstick. I'm not going to give her all my secrets because now that we are together again, I plan on using most of them on you myself. This bubble bath for two is one of them. I was hoping you showed up while I was in here. I wanted to do this," and she reached for his throbbing manhood and pulled on it stretching it toward her hot waiting mouth, the one that could bring Frank intense orgasms in seconds rather than the usual hour he liked to take. The other mouth, the hairy nether one would have to wait a bit longer.

∞∞∞∞∞

After his release, and after they bathe together, Carmen took Frank to look for their son in his room. "Doriano, I want you to meet Frank Marichelli, Simon's father. Frank this is Doriano," Carmen said leading the introductions of father to son.

"Ciao Mr. Marichelli. Come stai? Good to meet you. You've got a real basketball player on your hands in Simon. I saw him do a jump shot the other day and he looked like a pro. We played against each other on the neighborhood courts and he slammed dunked on me! I thought I was schooling him!"

Mr. Marichelli walked up and hugged Doriano to his chest. His son, who stood in front of him, was complementing his other son. It was amazing to Frank and the most amazing thing was that Doriano looked like him, the same strong jaw line, the same brows, wavy hair and even the eye color. He knew that the next time Doriano saw his own reflection in a mirror he would connect the dots and realize who they were to each other. For now he needed to discuss what they would tell him with Carmen, and there was no time right now. "It's good to meet you and thank you for taking an interest in my son. One day soon we'll all get together and shoot some hoops, but right now I need to pick up the other boys and the Hazelton girls from the music store. It sounds like you have the gift of languages, so are you also a music lover like the other kids seem to be?"

"Well, if in other kids you mean neighborhood friends, I would have to say not as much. I like the Jackson 5, and some of Ray Charles's stuff. I like James Brown and I think I can dance like Jackie Wilson, but I have no interest in playing an instrument," Doriano answered his father, not catching Frank's slip of the tongue. "Next year when I become a freshman, I plan on trying out for the basketball team, but we can talk more another time. Hope to see ya soon and it was a pleasure meeting you."

Frank looked over at Carmen and winked, relaying through that one move how proud he was of his son, and what he thought of her as a mother. She felt relieved that the meeting as friends first went smoothly, and winked back. After Frank left, Carmen asked Doriano what he thought of Frank. "So, son, what do you think of Frank? Is he at all like Simon?"

"Well, if the real question is what kind of father I think he'll make for me, I think he'll be happier now that he has you in his life, and that will trickle down to all of us."

Carmen was stunned and stood there with her mouth hanging open stupidly.

"You're gonna catch flies with your mouth open like that," her son told her, sounding just like an adult.

"Doriano! I'm speechless! How did you guess so soon?"

"Children aren't as clueless as most adults think we are. I knew that Ashford wasn't my real dad, regardless of what he thought. So, when do I get to meet the rest of the family?"

"I'm not sure son, but your father and I will try and make it soon. Maria is not going to take this well, I would imagine, but unless she wants to be a divorcee`, she'll have to come around to the truth. I knew Frank as a teenager, and all through college we were lovers. We've wanted to be together for a long time but because of my one error in judgment, we couldn't be. I have kept you and him apart, for that I'm truly sorry and apologize. Can you forgive me?"

"Yes, you are my mother and I forgive you. When I make mistakes, you are always ready to forgive me."

"I love you son," Carmen said while pulling Doriano into her arms. "Sleep tight."

While lying on her bed, hoping to get a call from Frank, Carmen thought over the day and how she and Frank almost missed each other. She was relieved that Rico wanted his father to meet her and wanting him involved in his music. Children were much easier than parents she thought. Now to face Maria.

Chapter Eight

Several days later, Tawnie and Bryen were signing up for the recital in a Chicago suburb in two weeks. Rico knew he wasn't ready to play in front of an audience, but he wanted to go and set up equipment, so he signed up too. "Tawnie, sit with me on the bus, alright," Bryen asked her.

"I will, Bry. Save me a seat if I get there after you, and I'll do likewise. Will you have a parent chaperone coming?"

"As far I know my dad was talking about coming. He said he's getting a hotel room though and won't stay with us kids at the college dorms. What about you, a parent chaperone?"

"No. They said with one of your parents going, the university staff and dorm attendants, there should be enough chaperones. They said they trust us," Tawnie said winking at Bryen.

"Do you think they should?"

"Um! Well that sounds like a challenge. Bry, are you challenging me to something?"

"Well the dorm has a swimming pool. I bet you won't go down after everyone's in bed and swim with me?"

"I'll bring my suit. Are you walking home today?"

"No, my dad's coming to discuss Rico and his instrument with Mrs. Ashford. Ciao, bella."

"Ciao Bry."

∞∞∞∞∞∞

"Rico, we wanted to let you choose your instrument today. I had Mrs. Ashford rent one of each, so whichever one you want we'll give you thirty days with, and after that you can let her know to return the other one. Within the thirty days, you can play on both here and at home, switching between the two, but on day 30, she will return one, okay son?"

"Okay, and grazie pops! Thanks Mrs. Ashford for your patience with me. I won't let either of you down. While you two discuss it, I'll take the trumpet and go play it on the tennis courts. I saw Simon and Doriano out there, and Bry went out there to wait for us. Ciao, Mrs. Ashford."

"Bueno sera Rico."

After Rico left, Frank took Carmen's hand and led her into her private cloak room, the one place at school she could see him if they were discussing the children and their music. He pulled her into his chest and started his loving of her by sucking on her bottom lip, which he could not get enough of, and licking her mouth. Carmen went straight for his belt buckle and undid his pants, and pulled out his humongous bullet shaped cock. This prize was what she couldn't get enough of, and felt empty when he was not around to share in her daily life and to make love to at night. She massaged him while trying to come up with some kind of arrangement that would satisfy everyone.

"Frank, my love, I am missing you still, even though we are in the same town now. What can we do; I need you so?"

"I know baby, I'm not happy with this either. Let's go together to Maria after we leave here and discuss it. We'll send the boys to the movies just in case she freaks out. For now, let me sink deep inside you, bella. I want to taste you baby, so sit up here on this bookcase, and I'll sit on this chair. Give me your panties, and raise your skirt. Lean back a bit, cara mia, I want to see your sweet lips. Ooooh, you shaved it bare for me, my sweet sweet girl. Pretty, so pretty." And Frank dove in. He lapped and sucked with his huge tongue, battering Carmen's hidden grape-like nubbin until it stuck its head out like a shy turtle cowering in its shell. Frank was determined that it would come out and breathe some air, and he went to work to make it happen. "Put your legs up here on the back of the chair, and spread'em as far as you comfortably can. Papa is going for that rich treasure you got hidden down in there. Tesoro mia, vita mia, mine alone. Say it Carmen, I want to hear you say it."

"Ahhh, all yours Frank, per sempre tua, per sempre tuaaaaaaaa!" Carmen sang out in passion. Frank was hitting all the right spots with that weapon of a tongue in his mouth, as she manipulated the one between his legs. "Ti amo, Frank, Amo solo te, Frank. Si, Si, Si Frank. Yes, take all that sweet juice, it's only for you.

It's longed for only you," she whispered as she poured all she had out onto Franks tongue.

"Thinking of you Carmen, that's all I do. Tell me I'm all you'll ever need. This is mine, only for me. Our love is stronger than it's ever been. All night, Carmen, I want to be with you all night, and after we talk to Maria, I'll go back and stay with you tonight. It'll turn out right, as long as we stick together. Ummmm, pull that thing. Now, I'm going to turn you around and sink in the back, like we did last time."

Frank was overly stimulated and dying to dive deep, and with Carmen's cries and moans he buried himself into the one place he could stay forever, and would give up everything for if he had to. He didn't think Maria would want to be alone raising six rambunctious boys, so he didn't think he'd have too much trouble with her. He just hoped Carmen would never leave him again.

"Carmen, tell me you'll never leave me again. Don't get this wrong, but I'll never let you go again. I love this girl, and I love this too much to see it gone. This is mine, and everything you are is mine. Tell me you are mine," he pounded into her ass rocking deep, talking gibberish; he was ensnared and never wanted to be released from her trap. "Fly Carmen, you can have your freedom to fly, but you best know you won't go without me, cause I love it, I love it, and I need it. I need you, cara mi, mi bellaaaaaa, aaahhhh, aahh, awwwww!" and Frank shattered into a thousand pieces.

∞ ∞ ∞ ∞

Frank picked up the boys from the tennis court and followed Carmen to her house to drop off her car. He told her, either way he was driving her back to her house that night; that, no matter what Maria decided, he would stay with her tonight. When Frank walked in to his house, he smelled that dinner was ready, and hoped he could sit down and enjoy a quiet meal surrounded by the people who he loved most in the world. He planned on explaining this to his family, and hoped that they would be able to sense his sincerity because he wanted them all together for the rest of their lives. He went into the dining room and found Maria setting the salad bowls down. "Ciao bella."

"Hey you! Who ya got with you?" she asked smiling and leaned into him for a kiss.

"Company for dinner, and after we eat I'm sending all the fella's to the movies while we talk. Will that be okay with you?"

"Of course Frank; whatever you want. Hello Mrs. Ashford, and who is this handsome man? My god Frank, he looks like you. What'd you do find a relative in that school Simon?"Maria asked innocently, having no suspicions.

"Something like that. He does look like pop, almost more than some of these guys. They must take after your side of the family mama, huh?" Simon said, pointing at his younger brothers.

"Yes, Frankie looks like one of my brothers, Lorenzo looks like my father, Mario looks like Frank with dark skin and blue eyes, Bryen looks like Gregory Peck and Rico a young Tyrone Powers. I guess you look like me, Simon, fairer than most Italians and this young man looks like Frank and Mario. Everyone run wash so we can eat."

"Well, we can all get to know each other either this visit or next time. Can I help you with anything?" Carmen asked Maria wanting to change the subject.

"Yes, come on in the kitchen. Frank I'll grab a beer for you, have a seat, we'll be right out."

"Good, I can use a drink. Get one for Carmen too."

"Oh, it's Carmen already, huh?" Maria asked laughing at her husband as the two women headed into the kitchen.

In the kitchen Maria told Carmen, "I have an outfit I bought for tonight that I want to show you. I also bought 4 inch heels and some red lipstick. I have a seduction planned for Frank, so after the boys leave come upstairs with me, okay?"

"Sure."

"How did Rico perform today?"

"He did well, and chose the trumpet and saxophone to try for thirty days. Ummm, that smells delicious. Is it lasagna?"

"Yes, I got the recipe from Frank's sister. Do you know any of them?"

"Not really," Carmen admitted, but didn't want to say more. She knew all about the father, and she was the reason Frank was kicked out of his home.

"Well, I guess that's it for dinner preparations. You want to grab a drink for yourself and I'll offer water, cool-aid and lemon-aid to the boys."

"I'll take a glass of red wine. Shall I bring the bottle?"

"Yes, because I'll take a glass too. If you get Frank, I'll call the boys," Maria said running up the back stairs.

Frank heard Maria, and came up behind Carmen and kissed her on the back of the neck, and reached around and caressed her nipples. Then he held out the chair for her and they sat down at the dining table and looked at each other, until the others poured into the room. "So fella's, what movie do you want to see? I'm paying for the popcorn too, so make a choice?"

"True Grit, Butch and Sundance, Ben Hur!" all came out in a chorus."

"Ok, well you can flip a coin and that's the one for this week, and if chores get done, behavior stays on course then maybe next weekend you can all go see the one not chosen this week, okay?" Frank announced the way it would go.

"Ok pops," was what he heard.

The ladies got excited when Frank did his job as a father, and they loved him for it and the way he included all of the boys. For Carmen, she loved his ability to listen to and really hear what each son said. For Maria, she loved his ability to compromise and problem solve to the satisfaction of all, and soon both women would be tested on how they accepted his decisions with regards to their relationship as a threesome.

∞∞∞∞∞

After Frank returned from taking the boys to the theatre, he called Carmen and Maria in from the kitchen and after they each found a chair facing Frank he began with, "Maria, you are a good mother to my sons and I thank you for loving them. I want to be honest with you about us though, you and I and it's no reflection on you, it's all me. When you and I met I was in mourning and heartbroken over the loss of another woman. I had just returned to college from a funeral, the funeral of Carmen's mother. Carmen and I fell in love in high school, and because of circumstances we could not work it out to either of our satisfaction."

Maria gasped when he said Carmen's name, and she looked at Carmen.

"Carmen returned to college also, but she went back carrying my son. The young man you met today is indeed my son, and I'm telling you now because you already noticed the similarities in our appearance, and we want you to be the first to know. I have missed the first fourteen years of his life, and Maria my choice is to be in his life for the rest of it, and I hope you can understand that. I want to hear your thoughts so far as to what I'm telling you."

"I heard you say that you and Carmen know each other, and have known each other intimately for years," Maria cried out inaccurately. "Ohhhhh, Frank, have I been a substitute for Carmen all these years?"

"Not quite, Maria. Carmen and I were just reunited several weeks ago, when Rico decided to choose between the trumpet and saxophone. I hadn't seen her for fourteen years, and I didn't know about Doriano until that night. Carmen is my first love, and we promised each other that we would try and be together forever. I care about you, and I want to be around for the raising of my sons. I have a solution and I think it will work if we allow it to, and put the boys first. Is it true you and Carmen get along and are friends?"

"Yes, up to this point. Now, I don't know. Am I going to have to compete for your love Frank? I do know one thing about you, and that is that your ass is spoiled! You are one spoiled bastard Frank!" she yelled at him, her voice filled with anguish.

"I accept that Maria, and no, there will be no competing. I think we can all live in harmony and love each other in order to raise these boys in love and to help them grow to be productive citizens. I'm suggesting that we keep this quiet, but that we move in together, all of us under one roof. We'll have to work out a schedule between the three of us. I know it's unconventional but it's been done, and is being done in this country every day. I won't expect you to make a decision right away, but sleep on it and let me know. Maria, this is something I need to do to keep my family together. For me and for Carmen there is no other decision and we're already on the same page about it. I know it might be a shock to you right now, but if you think back to the time we met, were getting to know each other, you will remember I was distant with you. It was because of Carmen, and if truth be told it will always be Carmen." Frank looked over at Carmen, and they smile at each other.

"Carmen, are you really okay with everything Frank is saying? You wouldn't mind sharing him with me?"

"Maria, I have been in love with Frank since my junior year in high school. He was my first love and lover, the one who popped my cherry. He lived with my family, above our garage and used to sneak in my bedroom window at night. We have an unbreakable bond and now with our son, it's even stronger. We hate that we've had to be apart for so many years because we promised a lifetime of devotion. It's mostly my fault, but we promised not to blame each other, which would be looking back and we want to look forward, spend time loving. I can accept you and your six sons as an extension of my family, because I don't have anyone but Frank and Doriano. Maria, it's easy for me to love, my heart is open to love, and I want to give Frank more children. Personally, I would be happy to share a home with you since I enjoy your company and I love the children. If you can open your mind to the possibilities, I think we can have a wonderful life together as a family. Maybe we can buy a property out in the country away from prying eyes. The boys will be driving soon, and that will be a big help."

"Maria, you would always know where I am at night. I would be in your bed or Carmen's or down the hall from you. I think we can each have a room, one that the children would believe is my room alone, and on every other night I would be with one of you, even if it's just to sleep. We could take turns with the babies when they come, and take turns going on trips with the older ones and their music. If you one day find that you are unhappy, if you feel that love has somehow made you a fool, feel free to try something new, but I don't think you will find anything better. Like I said, no pressure, just know that we are on the same page already." And he pointed at himself and Carmen.

"You have given me a lot to think about. One thing I already know is that I would be very unhappy apart from my boys, and even if I am a little hurt and angry with you right now, I would miss being apart from you for too long. I don't think I have much choice, but I'll sleep on it tonight. I assume you and Carmen will be together tonight?"

"Yes, I'm going to pick up the boys, probably let Simon stay with Doriano and stay at Carmen's tonight. Can you pack a bag for Simon please? We'll see you sometime tomorrow. Can I kiss you goodnight, bella?" And Maria walked into his arms and he held her for a minute. "Bueno sera."

Chapter Nine

Maria, at first struggled with the relationship, and Frank understood. She needed time and Frank allowed her some private time, and took Carmen and the boys to the recital, but allowed Rico and Bryen to ride the bus with the other musicians since they were a part of the schools team. The recital, held outside Chicago was a two-day event with children from schools across the state participating. This year the schools chose themed music from movies that were blockbusters, and because Carmen's group performed Butch Cassidy and the Sundance Kid's so well locally, she chose that for her group. All the schools children were staying in the host college empty dorm rooms because all the college kids had left for spring break. Carmen, as a teacher didn't have to stay with her students so she stayed with Frank at a local hotel, along with the youngest and oldest boys.

On the trip up to the host city Bryen sat with Tawnie and Rico sat in the seat across the aisle. He held his sax in his lap and practiced while serenading her with love songs from various artists, and one that was her favorite was from a French movie translated Endless Love. Tawnie was shocked at how quickly Rico had picked up the basics and how well he played the instrument. He blew out notes from The Commodores Sail On, and Three times a Lady and she clapped when he finished; of course Bryen sat next to her steaming, and she could almost see the smoke rise from off of his body. She caressed his hand and whispered to him and either what she said or the movements of her hand soothe him, calming him.

After the recital, the kids were allowed to go to the pool to celebrate their performances and kick off the start of spring break. That night Bryen knocked on the door to Tawnie's dorm room and she came out in a fluorescent pink bikini. Bryen could not believe his eyes. She was filling out nicely, just like a real woman he thought. Soon, maybe in high school he would get her a promise ring and ask her to be exclusively his. Tawnie pulled the ribbon out of her hair and shook it. The texture was wavy and crinkled, but still hung down her back. Bryen reached out his hands and rubbed through it. He liked touching her and as they rode down the elevator, he pulled her close to his body. "Tawnie, I want to kiss you. May I?"

"Of course Bry." She stepped into his arms, he bent his head, and they kissed softly, lightly for a long time, her full lips trembling beneath his. Tawnie had been practicing on her own arm for this day, the day that Bry would ask to kiss her. She knew it would come, and that day was now and she was thrilled. They got down to the pool level, and jumped in holding hands. For the first hour or so, they swam laps, but reaching the point of exhaustion, they held onto the side of the pool and talked about their futures. Then Bry leaned into her and kissed her again, this time he didn't stop at just the soft peck, he did what he had been practicing, and licked her mouth and pulled her mouth open with his hand and rubbed his fingers inside her mouth. He'd seen this done in a movie recently, and at first Tawnie backed up, displacing his finger, but he did it again and she let him, knowing this was her Bry and he wouldn't hurt her. He rubbed it around in her mouth, around her tongue and teeth, not realizing that adults did this move as foreplay, a preamble to full-blown intercourse. He thought the man just wanted to feel her rough teeth against his finger, but he began to feel something in his lower body. He had begun having dreams of Tawnie and himself in a position like this, and he would wake up having shot cum in his underwear. He knew this was the first signs of puberty in a boy his age. He rubbed slowly, and she began to suck his finger and he reached for her around the waist. She then stuck her finger in his mouth, mimicking what he had done, and he sucked her finger. Then Rico dove in the pool and swam over to them. They broke apart and began playing tag. Rico had missed it, child's play that would soon lead to seduction.

Later, in separate beds and separate rooms, Tawnie and Bry both thought back over what had happened between them. They each felt changed; odd that just finger to mouth play could make them feel that they belonged to the other more than felt they had before. They knew that soon high school and then college would bring them together more and they wondered what that would lead to. They were both anxious to grow up, and it could not get here fast enough to suit them.

∞∞∞∞∞

While they were away on spring break, Frank used this time to let the boys know what was going on in the family. He was honest with them and told them that Carmen was as much his first wife as Maria was there mother. That he had intended to marry Carmen, but that her father and his stood in their way, preventing it. He knew his boys and just as he predicted, explaining it slowly and draped in love, they were able to understand. They had seen the loving relationship between Maria and him so when he showed love to Carmen they accepted it without question. She was the epitome of class and they liked her, and soon would love her as much as their own mother.

They all stayed together spread out within three rooms, and had a fun-filled spring break. Maria was home coming to terms with everything. On their way home, while everyone slept in the car, Frank used that time to look for a house out in the country, one big enough for a few additional children that Carmen would give him, children that should have been born almost thirteen years ago. He suspected that one would be on its way within the next six months since he found it hard to stay away from Carmen. Their loving was explosive and burned hotter than lava. Each time he came down from the highest heights he wanted to go right back up again. She was one of a kind.

Several weeks later, during the month of March 1969, with all the family together, Frank drove them out in the country to check out a house he'd found. The area they were in was lovely Carmen thought and there was a lot of space for breathing room, for the family to grow. They passed cows and horses, several farms and a creek or pond. It looked like a small village they passed about ten minutes back, nestled in a picturesque valley. There were hills, rivers and she saw several children skating on a pond. The snow was still covering the trees and the boys agreed that it would be fun to skate on a real pond like that. It seemed like they were close enough to seek medical attention if necessary, but still far enough away to ensure complete privacy from objecting elements; people could be so nosy. After about ten minutes, Frank turned down a large driveway that was lined with oaks, just like in the old south. He pulled up to a three-story farm house that had a wrap-a-round porch already outfitted with a porch swing and rocking chairs. Maria asked, "Is someone living here Frank?"

"You can be if you like it," he said grinning at her. "Everybody out, take a look around outside first, then we'll all go in together."

The boys ran off to check out the back lawn and area surrounding the huge house. Carmen was just as excited to explore as they were. Frank took both women in his arms and said, "Thank you my loves for making this easier than I thought it would be. Especially you Maria; I'm proud of you for believing in me and this family, having no expectations other than that because we love each other, we can make this work."

"I do believe in you, and I love you and because I'd rather be with you than without you, I knew there was only one decision I could make. Now what about this beautiful house, are you serious? We might be able to get it?"

"We have gotten it! What do you think Carmen, do you like it too?"

"Oh Frank! It's gorgeous. Can we afford it?"

"Yep, I already put a deposit down, and the owner just had it cleaned out. It wasn't even on the market yet. One of the engineers from work told me about it, and the old man who owned it was happy to know there would be plenty of boys to grow up in it. I told him about our clan and that there was probably a few more coming in the near future."

"Why did he sell Frank, did he say?" Carmen asked while glancing around her in amazement.

"His wife of fifty-five years has dementia and had to be moved into a nursing facility, so he moved in with her. Now that's love. Which one of you will move in with me if that happens?" he asked his two women half kidding, and half not.

"We both will I imagine," she smiled looking at Carmen, who nodded her head. "But with all the children we have and will have there will be no need to move you, because if we aren't able to take care of you one of them with their wife will. It'll probably be Bryen and Tawnie. That reminds me, maybe we should have something written up and notarized by the attorney regarding that point."

"Yeah Frank, mi corazone, if we wear you out, where will we be?" Carmen chuckled teasingly.

"I'll speak to the attorney when I meet with him about the house documents. I'll try and get him to meet us three together out here. So, how soon can you ladies pack?" he said grabbing them around their waists again.

They walked around the outside of the country house together arm in arm, exploring the sheds and barn, peeking around the area that would be used for a garden. Carmen moved rocks and a border fence that surrounded a spot that looked like it had been used just for herbs. She thought that would come in handy, the way she and Maria like to cook ethnic meals for their men. It would be fun to work together in what she imagined would be a huge kitchen and pantry area, hanging fresh herbs from the ceiling that they would grow themselves. Maria checked out a small building with a wire fence that she thought might have been a chicken coop, and could be once again housing chickens and hens in the near future.

Inside the barn was an old tractor, a bunch of tools hanging neatly on the walls and a lift where the previous owner might have worked on vehicles. With all males in the family and cars and trucks in abundance in their future, that would come in handy. Maybe one of them could train as a mechanic. Frank would have to steer a couple of them in that direction, and maybe one day they'd have their own mechanic in the family. Automotive repair bills were something they knew would be in abundance soon, in a family this size. Right now they needed a new larger station wagon, but since it was rare that they all piled in and rode together, having Carmen's car and Maria's car was helpful. On they walked until they came to the orchard. "Wow, an orchard too; I hope there's peaches, but any fruit we can grow would be a bonus for this family. The grocery bills have always been large, but will only get bigger. Carmen, once you find out you're pregnant, will you work until your due date?" Maria asked concerned.

"I did with Doriano, but it'll be up to Frank. I'm glad to leave major decisions in his hands now aren't you?"

"Yes, I usually do. With my first pregnancy, Frank didn't care if I worked or not, so I kept working until I went into labor. With Rico I went into premature labor and had to take forced retirement. After that, with a baby almost every year, it didn't pay to go out and work so I stayed home, and sometimes watched the neighbor's children for a few dollars of pin money. I have an idea, that I want to run by you and Frank," Maria told Carmen. "I'll bring it up once we get back to the house."

"Okay, I'll try and remember to remind you. Rico is really getting good at the saxophone. We have another recital coming up in a couple of weeks at the school. Do you plan on going or will Frank? I think Rico is ready to be a part of the group number. He won't have that much music, but the experience will be invaluable."

"I'm not sure. We could all go if there's nothing planned except that. Let's discuss it with Frank later. You know with this size of a garden we could put in everything; what kind of veggies would you want to grow? I already know that I'll want snap peas."

Carmen put one hand on her hip and the other on her chin in thought and said, "Hmmm. I love tomatoes, corn on the cob, any kind of lettuce other than iceberg, and all kinds of greens, especially collards and mustards."

"Hey you two, come join us, we're heading into the house. We can come back any time, we own it!" Frank smirked.

∞ ∞ ∞ ∞

The boys were exploring the upstairs and attic, trying to decide which room they wanted for their own. Simon and Dariano thought they wanted to share the attic or basement. Maria and Carmen were still in the foyer, taking in the dark wood paneling, high ceilings and the huge heavy doors. Fascinated, they moved from one room to the other, as they all seem to connect down here, leading into the kitchen. The dining room had a picture window that begged to be looked out, to view the woodlands beyond the side yard. Maria's eyes grew wide as she took in the countertops and flooring of the roomy kitchen. The seat under the bay window would be a dream to sit in and read on rainy days watching the garden grow. The walls were cream with blue bells and corn flowers painted around the midline. All they would have to do in here is move in the most modern refrigerator, put the deep freeze out in the pantry and add tables and chairs. There was a bathroom off the pantry, for the kids to use in emergencies coming from outside with mud on themselves. There was even an office that they could use to sit and discuss meal planning or their schedules for the three adults. Frank could be heard moving around in his boots, and finally they heard him on the landing calling for them, "Come check out the master bathroom. You're gonna flip. The old guy must've worked in tile, and sure knew what he was doing."

The ladies reached the bathroom and their eyes popped wide when they saw how luxurious everything was. The bathroom was done in pale green marble, with silver taps and a large round bathtub. Above the sink was a mirror that appeared to be carved out of the same marble but had added ivory tiles from the tusk of elephants. Wow, was too small a word for what Carmen felt she wanted to express. She was blown away by the detail in this place. It seemed like it was done as a labor of love from a man to his life love, and that's how she felt knowing that Frank bought it with her in mind. Well, with her and Maria in mind, she added generously. From now on, everything would be shared and would be us, we three. Moving on into the master bedroom, the room designed for a couple and would now hold maybe three sometimes, the ladies looked at and felt the drapes that hung magnificently from the windows that were overlarge to show off the entire back lawn, even down to the orchards. The drapes were heavy brocade and were inlaid with seed pearls combined with embroidery. Frank could picture a new enormous four-poster bed with draping around it to match the ones at the windows that would give him extra privacy when he wanted to make love. "Hey pops, come check out the paintings hidden in the attic, Doriano called from the stairway!"

The three adults moved up the hallway to the stairs that led to the attic, and stopped when they saw all the paintings that were hung on the walls. They each had a tag on them with the name of the painting printed on it. These were beyond wonderful, but were museum quality. They looked like they were part of a heist. Carmen would have to do research, not believing that the owners were artist, but that would make sense. Who else could afford the luxury they were looking at, other than a truly talented genius in a genre of art of one kind or another? "Frank, did you get the previous owners name. I think we should research him, or her? Do you think he meant to leave all these here?"

"I think so. Where would he take them moving into the nursing facility? Maybe he had a sale, sold everything and forgot these were here. We could find out where he moved to and go and see him and his wife. Maybe take them some pasta and wine?"

"Aww, baby, that is so sweet! Let's do that just because we appreciate the magnificence of this house that he took such good care of," Carmen said, shedding a tear.

"Now don't you start that, cara mia." Frank told her, leaning in to her and swiping his tongue across the tears and licking them from her face like a puppy.

"You two are so tenderhearted," Maria said laughing. "I will make the pasta, Carmen you pick out the wine and do the salad. But right now, let's go see the other rooms," Maria exclaimed excitedly leading them back down the stairs.

The next room that the adults would use had a white door, and behind it was a room that the couple evidently did not use, because everything was a pristine white with gold trim. The drapes were again the heavy brocade that was probably custom made to order as were the ceiling moldings and baseboards. The walls were covered in a paper edged in gold. They had even left the bed, which was a four-poster and big. It had covers that looked soft, expensive and was left fully made. The wardrobes for clothing were hand carved and trimmed in colors matching the drapes, and the clothes closets were deep and large enough to hold the clothing from several others. "Where is the nursery, Frank?" Carmen asked gently.

Frank looked at her wide-eyes saying, "Why?"

Carmen said, "No babe. Nothing yet but soon though."

"No rush." Frank smiled and winked at his love. "When she does make her appearance, she will know that she was wanted and longed for. The nursery is down here near the third adult bedroom with windows that face the side and back lawn. Let's get it painted for a girl and outfitted with girly stuff."

"Whatever you say vito mio," Carmen whispered blowing him a kiss.

Frank opened the door to a very pretty little room that shouted "a precious baby girl" rooms here. It was a soft white and had buttercups painted around the midline. There was a window seat built in and dressers and a wardrobe too. The closet was a good size, and the most wonderful thing was there was a built in bathroom and a chute leading down to the laundry room, which they knew was thoughtfully installed for a busy mother. The ladies ooh and aah over this room and knew they'd love to spend lots of time here nursing their babies from the breasts. A rocking chair facing the window to watch the sunrise would be perfect, and neither could wait to get pregnant.

"It's very pretty, baby," Carmen said caressingly. "I can't wait to bring our baby girl here and thank you for everything. This whole house is a treasure and I love it, right Maria?"

"I agree, and I think it's perfect for us and can't wait to move in. Our lives will change from this day forward, and I know it will all be positive and wonderful. Thank you sweetheart, and blew Frank a kiss."

Chapter Ten

Over the weekend, the family moved into their new country manor and worked hard to arrange all the furniture and put everything in its place. Each floor was equipped with an intercom so no more shouting up the stairs. The boys scattered throughout the third floor and basement. The attic they would leave empty for now until the other babies began to come.

On Sunday afternoon, while the fella's went in to town, Bryen to see what he could arrange about bringing Tawnie and several of her sisters out, and a stop in for mass for the others. The ladies stayed home and walked around the garden with a paper and pencil, some string and sticks to plot out specific areas that they wanted to plant. When they finished that they walked down to the orchard to see if it would need spraying for the season's next harvest. Then they mapped out an area between the garden and the orchard to see if there would be enough room to build an in-ground swimming pool for the boys. Because they were so far from town, the school, and any regular activities, the ladies wanted to gift the boys with a pool and basketball court. So together they worked to fulfill the plans and tried to come up with some ideas for a special gift for Frank. When they heard the fella's return they gathered up their supplies, locked them in the shed and walked back to the house.

Carmen was cooking tonight, but she had already put a roast to slow cook in the oven, and wanted to soak in a hot bubble bath for awhile. When she went into her bedroom, after stripping out of her dirty clothes and then on into her bathroom, she found rose petals and candlelight throughout. Frank was sitting naked waiting for her in the oversized tub. When he saw her, he reached for the stereo and put on Skylark's Wildflower. "Ciao bella, come stai?" he whispered.

"Buona Sera, mi amore, Io sono prego. Grazie, sei molto gentile," Carmen said caressingly back to Frank, easing her aching body into the water. It smelled so good. Frank evidently found her boxed bath soaps, because no way would he have anything in his own shaving kit that smelled this good. "Did the Hazelton girls come back with you guys? I wanted Tawnie to help Bry and Rico set up an area in the basement for a little music room with stands and chairs."

"Yep, so relax baby they're down there now arranging and rearranging. How are you precious? Any sign of my daughter yet? You sure do look pretty today. I like your hair in two braids like that; it reminds of high school when I followed you around, and you wouldn't give me the time of day or even notice me."

"Well my love, I made up for it didn't I?" Carmen purred, giggling. "And baby I see you now, you and your big fat cock. Baby, can you rub my shoulder a little lower on the right. I lifted the wheelbarrow trying to turn it."

"You did what! Carmen, don't do that! If you happen to be carrying my daughter, I would like for her to rest easy in there, and not be awakened to soon by your over enthusiasm in the garden, baby. I noticed that these remarkable tits are even fuller than normal, sweetheart. I think you're pregnant? As lovely as you are, you are glowing now. It's as if you're lit up from within and it has to be the baby."

"Can't it be because you make me so happy darlin? That Doriano and I are so blessed to have found you again, and doubly blessed that you would even look at me after . . ." Frank stopped her by grabbing her chin, then by cupping her breasts and sucking first one and then the other. He pulled on their oversized plump nipples, realizing even before she did that Carmen was indeed pregnant. She was as ripe and ready to be plunged into as he had ever seen her. He put her legs over the top of his tree-trunk-like thighs and eased her even closer to him in the water. She ran her hands through his hair, wetting it and started massaging his scalp, licking the drips of water that rained down. He moaned and so did she from what he was doing to her underneath the water. He had stuck his middle finger inside her velvety hair-covered lips and was reaching for her favorite spot. Back and forth he worked it and touched deep, hitting the smooth inner walls of her beautiful pussy. Frank was careful but wanted to bring her to climax, so he pulled the plug to release the water and lay her backwards, keeping a hold on her thighs. When she was fully stretched out, he put one thigh over his shoulder and opened her wide, and started slowly looking to draw out the "man in the boat" to come play. It didn't take long, and that to him was another good sign of her pregnancy. He stroked it, allowing his callused finger tip to brush up and down over the sensitive nub as lightly as a puff of air. He bent over and used his tongue to do what the finger tips started and battered the boatman good and worked it from within and without until he had her writhing, gasping and ultimately screaming. Then he lay on top of her and plunged deep. "How's that feel beautiful? You still love me?"

All she could do was squeeze with her thighs as a sign that she was hearing and coherent. It was wonderful for her, and she tingled and shivered, allowing the heat to spread over her and through her. She felt sensations that she had never felt before, and as Frank pummeled her wet nest, it only intensified until she was screaming again with a multiple orgasm. He came with her, purring Italian words of love in her ears. "Ahhhh, cara mia, mi amore, luce mia, per sempre insieme," he choked out through his own volcanic orgasm.

"Sei incredibile, Frank," she told him tearfully, feeling overly emotional at this moment. He reached out and grabbed a thick oversized bath towel and wrapped her in it, and held her while she cried.

∞∞∞∞∞

At dinner that night, with guests present, the boys were at their best. Bry pulled Tawnie's chair out for her, and Doriano took care of Aubree's. "Well young ladies, how do you like the new house?" Maria asked proudly.

"We love it!" both girls said together. "There is so much room, and with the large barn we wondered if you would have horses? I would love to bring the little ones out so they could ride?" Aubree shared.

"That's a good idea missy. I think we'll get a couple, especially since our little ones are sure to love horses." Frank said, wondering who would catch the hint.

"We already do pops!" Frankie said loudly. "Mama, next time we go into town can we bring Raina and Aslee out here to see the farm?"

"Is that how you see our new home Frankie, as a farm? We don't have any animals yet. What kind of animal do you want to get first, farmer Frankie," Maria teased her baby, ruffling his hair.

"I want two things mama; a goat for me, and a lamb for Raina. Will that be okay Pops? I want to surprise her the first time she comes and visits us."

"That sounds like a good idea Frankie. One day next week, on our way home we'll stop at the farms that we past and ask the real farmers if we can buy a goat and a lamb for Raina. Now if we were to get a couple mares and a stallion to keep'em company, which one of you would learn how to take care of them?"

"I would!" Doriano said first. "I also want to learn how to tear down cars, and of course to put'em back together."

"Sounds great son, we'll sure need a mechanic in the family. Next year you'll be able to take driver's ed, and along with that we'll set you up in a vocational ed program so you can do both at the same time. There's no sense in driving if you can't take care of a car." Frank told him.

"Fa sho, pops!" Doriano said.

"Simon, do you think caring for and maybe raising horses could be something you could get into; maybe make it a career, or did you have a plan for your life already? Now is the time to begin goal-setting and formulating a plan for your future. This property is big enough for all of you to get a piece of when the time comes to set up your own homes. I'd love to see some of you stick around so we can watch your children grow up around us."

"I might try and get a full ride to UCLA on a basketball scholarship, but I have to maintain my grade point average, which is no problem right now because I've been on the honor roll consistently so far," Simon told the family.

"Yes you have and we are all very proud of you. Keep up the good work. I think it's your turn to have me at your next game, right? Make sure you let me know and put it up on the calendar in the office by the pantry. We will have all appointments and events in there so we don't miss anything. One of us adults will be at every event you kids have, except when one of the ladies are in labor and delivering a new baby. Okay?"

All the kids spoke in one voice saying, "Okay pops!"

∞∞∞∞

After dinner, the Hazelton girls helped clean up and then went down into the basement to find the boys. The younger three were playing Monopoly, bragging about who had the most winnings, and Doriano and Simon were throwing darts. Bryen was tuning his cello and Rico was warming up the Sax, and asked, "Tawnie, come over her a minute. Can you put that next album on, the John Coltrane; I want to run through this piece of music following him. Aubree, why didn't you take lessons on an instrument?"

"At the time I wanted to dance, you know modern dance and follow in the footsteps of the greats like Merce Cunningham, Baryshnikov and even Fred Astaire. The greatest though in the type of flowing movements that I prescribe to was Isadora Duncan. She traveled all over the world dancing and trying to get people to see her vision and take up her philosophy of dance, that dance need not be restrictive and rigid as ballet is; that there is a connection between emotions and movement. Just like between music and emotions. Don't you play differently when you are in different moods? Anyone can move in a free-flowing way like she insisted on doing but ballet is like torture, and I don't know how it even became so popular since not everyone can do it. Can you imagine a fat girl being lifted up over some boy's head?" Aubree said speaking with passion.

"Brava, Aubree! You speak so passionately about dance. Are you dancing now?" Simon asked.

"Sometimes. Recently I had an idea to put on a dance recital, an entertainment feast that all of us kids can have a part in. The size of this basement makes me think that it will work as our stage and still have room for the audience, our parents and several of their friends. Each of us could highlight our talents and those who don't want to be out front could work behind the scenes working on props, lighting or even building the sets? What do you guys think? Do you think you'd like to put on a show to celebrate an event maybe at the beginning of summer? We'd probably need that much time to design the set, make the costumes and get the music prepared."

"I think it sounds like a wonderful idea!" Tawnie said excitedly, jumping up from her seat by the stereo. "Bryen, Rico what do you guys think? Can you work with Aubree as director of a night of entertainment for the folks?"

"I think so," Rico admitted, nodding his head. "I might need your help Tawnie with the music, but yeah it sounds like a blast."

"Bry, what do you think?" Tawnie looked at her best friend wanting his opinion mostly.

"Yeah, I think it sounds like fun. If they get the swimming pool built by then, we could all have a pool party afterwards."

"Aw yeah, I love swimming. I hope they get done, and maybe I'll invite some friends over." Doriano said getting involved in the excitement. "I'll tell our parents what we want to do, or is it a secret Aubree?"

"No, we're going to need help making the costumes, so I'll tell my parents."

"Oh, I meant to ask you two, do you know a Jay Mills?" Simon asked the girls.

"Yeah, he's our cousin, why?" Tawnie said before Aubree could get anything out.

"He told me to stay away from you two. I thought to myself what the heck is he talking about. I wondered if he was trying to talk to you himself. Now I think, he thought I was trying to date one of you, or that I would play you, but now I see he was just being a protective cousin. We're on the same basketball team, that's how I know him. Maybe I'll invite him over when we have the pool party and he can see for himself what's going on"

"That'll be nice. We don't see him or his sister much anymore since we moved over in the new neighborhood," Aubree said.

"We're going to miss seeing you guys down on the court shooting baskets," Tawnie said quietly.

"Well you might miss us down there, but that doesn't mean you won't see us because you can come here," Bryen piped in.

"It won't be the same because you were there practically every day, and we can't get out here every day," she responded.

"That's true, but absence makes the heart grow fonder, isn't that what they say?" Bryen volleyed back at her.

"Hmm! Well I can't wait until I can start driving myself around. I got places to go and people to see!" Tawnie joked.

"Well that'll come soon enough, missy, so slow ya roll!" Bryen warned her.

Tawnie looked at him and rolled her eyes, secretly loving his possessiveness. They may be young but they knew they were meant for each other already. "Put the record on and have a seat!" Bryen added. Thereafter, Tawnie did exactly as she was told. Everybody else looked at each other and shook their heads.

"Speaking about preparing food, Tawnie let's find Carmen and Maria and bake some practice cookies for everyone. Do you guys have chocolate, vanilla, eggs and butter?"

The guys looked at each other, hunched their shoulders, shook their heads and the girls knew they didn't know, so they ran up the steps to find the ladies. Later they brought the fresh baked cookies still warm from the oven down to the basement. While they ate, they drank chilled milk. The guys showed appreciation by gobbling them all up.

Chapter Eleven

Later that week, Carmen scheduled an appointment with her OBGYN to get an exam and pregnancy test. The next day she received the call that Frank longed to hear; he had guessed correctly by feel and sight that they were pregnant. For now, Carmen wanted the news to be kept quiet because she was over thirty and was not sure if she was at risk for miscarriage or not. Frank and Maria agreed to stay mum, and wait at least until the fourth month. It was extremely hard to not shop though, so Maria and Carmen met for lunch at the weekend and went shopping at every infant boutique they could find. They promised each other to hide their findings in the baby's closet and they set a limit on each other. Maria bought pale yellow and green yarn that she planned on knitting into an afghan for the baby regardless of its gender. Carmen bought booties in white and a sweater in pink and white, hoping for a girl. The ladies snuck in the house when they returned home and ran to hide the little treasures in the baby's room closet, giggling all the way there and back down stairs to the kitchen, where they found Frank sitting in the window seat reading the paper and keeping an eye on the contractor installing the pool.

Everyone was excited about the pool and a few of the boys began taking swimming lessons so that they would be ready to spend the summer at poolside. Bryen knew it was a way to get his friends the Hazelton's over almost every day. He asked Mr. Hazelton if there was a way to get the girls out to the country for most of the summer and Mr. Hazelton told him that they would try to come up with a plan. It was too far to ride bikes, there was no bus that went out that far, and the boys were too young to drive, so it would be up to the adults. During the pool install, several men from the same crew poured concrete for a basketball court and Maria suggested that they have the men set up an area for the soon to arrive babies. Carmen thought a jungle gym with infant swings and slides to start with, and graduate to different sizes as the little ones grew, would be nice and practical. They were setting the boys up to spend most of their time at home with their own family and not running the streets, so they were making sure they had plenty of activities and equipment.

Maria asked Frank if she could talk to them both about a plan she wanted to try, but first she needed to know a few things, so she started by telling them what she wanted," I'd like to return to work while Carmen is home over the summer with the boys. Now that we are expecting, I doubt that she will want to return to the school, at least full time once the baby arrives. By the way, did you get a deliver date?" she turned to look at Carmen.

"October, right before Halloween," Carmen answered.

"Wow, honey, you will be uncomfortable in the heat of summer, but we have central air so during the warmest part of the day I expect you to stay indoors, okay?" Frank counseled.

"Yes my love. The boys will be swimming, so I will probably need a cabana area or gazebo with a lounger in it to escape the sun, but still be available for them. We could hook up some ceiling fans and a small cooler to keep drinks and popsicles for all of us. But more about summer, let' continue with what Maria wants to do. Maria, where do you want to put your nursing degree to use; a hospital, the school, a nursing facility, or have you given it much thought?"

"I thought I would start with a nursing agency, one that I could pick up hours across all medical fields or genres, maybe starting as an on-call nurse. That way I can reestablish myself, build my confidence back up and begin anew. I've been out of practice for almost thirteen years and will probably need a refresher course. While Carmen is still early in her pregnancy, I was thinking I had better do it now, that way over the summer while she's home, she might need me to be around here to help keep an eye on things. I will only pick up shifts while you're home in the evenings Frank. I think I should start out as I plan to go, that way everyone can get use to a routine. In the fall, when the kids go back to school I want to be there for them, so I was thinking I would apply now to the school district so that by then I will be ready to jump right in. I can take all the big kids to their building and then roll over to the elementary school, work until the older kids get out, and then roll back and pick up the young ones. I could stay at the elementary school nursing office just until Frankie moves up. Then, unless I get pregnant, I'll go back on call. I can still get pregnant too. I've been on the pill, and plan on staying on it until after Carmen has this baby, then we'll see. Although, once baby girl shows up and keeps us all up at night, I might change my mind."

"Oh uh uh! Did she just insult my fetus," Camen asked laughing. They all laughed, knowing it was probably going to be true. For all of them, it had been awhile since there was an infant in the house.

"Well, it sounds like you've worked it out in your own mind rather well, dear. That's why I'm attracted to you two, you're so organized. I just have to love you and bring home my paycheck, and you do the rest. Is that what you need me for?" he asked smirking at his two women.

"Yeah!" the two chorused at him, and they all laughed hard. Then the two women jumped up from their chairs and fell onto Frank, while all three continued laughing.

Later that night, Frank visited Maria in her room. She was waiting for him, decked out in her cocktail waitress costume, pumps and red lipstick; her body radiant with a lightly scented oil. "Aw Big Daddy, you are in trouble now!" she purred, striking a pose in her get up. "What good dish can I serve you tonight? We have two kinds of lips, both smooth and ready to please. We have two plump delicious breasts, or how about a choice piece of thick hot juicy ass vita mio?"

"Wow, il tuo corpo e` bellissimo, mi fai eccitare, Maria. I think I'll take a little taste of all the choices offered."

"Whatever you desire mi amore, this is your night." Maria bent over giving Frank a look at her pushed up tits, and then turned around and bent over again and shook her backside at him, bringing her hand down hard and slapping her own cheek. The sound reverberated through the room, making Frank's cock throb and tremble beneath his sateen pajama bottoms. He pulled them off and stretched out on the bed. He began massaging his own huge dick and waving it toward Maria. She sauntered over to the bed, kicked off her pumps and reached for him. She took him in her hands and stroked him, drawing moans from his lips. She pulled her lacy costume up over her olive tinged creamy thighs, exposing her smooth perfectly shaved nether lips that seemed to whisper to Frank "open the package and find the surprise" so he reached for it with the tips of his rough over-sized beefy hands and caressed it. Maria was in a teasing playful mood, so she scooted away from his hands and ran her own up her groin and toward her labia lips and squeaked out a gasp, squirming around the bed as she brushed her hooded clit. She opened and closed her legs, teasing Frank and making him hard as steel. She wanted to hear him beg for it, so she mischievously exposed her glistening pink meat, arching her back and raised her legs in the air to do a little air dance. Frank watched in the shadowed room, with just the light from the full moon shining through the open drapes.

"Very pretty, cara mia. May I touch it again?" Frank asked, but not quite in the begging tone that Maria especially wanted to hear, so she made him wait. She wanted him overly stimulated so that just a few pumps would take him to the pinnacle of ecstasy, giving him something that he would not soon forget. She knew that Carmen had to be an excellent lover in order to have kept his interest for so long, and she wanted to do the same. So she drew out the seduction saying, "Oh Big Daddy, baby's been a bad girl and needs some of your training," in a high squeaky voice. She then flipped over onto her knees and turned around, putting her ass cheeks in his face. She shook it, reaching back with her hands and opened her cheeks up to expose her back hole. Frank moaned low deep in his gorgeous throat, sounding like a hungry wildcat on the hunt, and reached out his hands for her. Maria asked him, "Are you begging for?"

"Yes, and taking it," and slammed her down on his engorged shaft, that stood up like a pole. She screamed, unprepared for the assault that he waged on her body. "Is this what baby wanted, to be pummeled and masticated by Big Daddy's rod? Is this what baby likes? It's what Big Daddy likes." Frank had stamina and rocked her world, driving himself into her deep, until she could not take another orgasm, already laughing and crying at the same time. She crawled away from him, leaving him stiff but she was not about to leave him unsatisfied. She turned her body around, straddled him backwards and went to work with her mouth, dragging her tongue and lips around his swollen blood-filled cock. All the while Frank murmured sweet nothings in both Italian and English saying, "That's right little girl, work Big Daddy good. Suck that long dong, you can do. It's all for you sweet thang. Make it cum, cause you can do it, you're sooo good at it darling girl, daddy's precious little darling." It did not take long before he shouted out his release; shooting off down her throat.

Chapter Twelve

Before they knew it, summer was in full swing, school was out and Carmen's baby bump showed nicely under her new maternity smocks. Frank could not let her pass him without reaching out and rubbing her tummy where his seed had taken root. He was thrilled and hoped for a little girl that looked just like Carmen with a dash of his good looks too.

Maria was working in the evenings after Frank got home, Simon and Dariano were taking drive's ed all summer so they worked hard in the evenings to get the stage built for the big family dance and music recital that their friends were sewing costumes for. Carmen even made programs and invitations that she planned on mailing out to their closest friends. Aubree as director assumed that plans were coming together nicely. She figured that instead of anyone cooking for the event, she would order large pizzas to have delivered and she would bake cookies and have a choice of drinks to pass around. For weeks, the young people got together in the basement and backyard to practice the music so that the moves and music coordinated and flowed flawlessly. Tawnie would play piano for several numbers that Aubree danced too, but Aubree asked that she also make up a dance to perform as a solo. It was suggested that the kids plan on two set ups, one for the basement in case it rained, and one for the back lawn for good weather. Lighting had been installed around the finished pool and it looked spectacular. The gardens were in full bloom and perfumed the air with scents of lilac and roses. The ladies had planted calla lily bulbs right after they moved in and they were blooming and stood tall and straight as sentinels guarding a fortress.

The youngest of the siblings made silver stars from foil to hang around the trees and bushes and to stick in the ground on stakes. They would also have a part in the performances so they were together a lot practicing their pieces. Raina planned on reciting a poem, Aslee wanted to twirl her baton and do a rodeo routine while decked out in a western costume. She had even found a pair of white cowboy boots in a thrift store to wear for the evening. Trina, the tall awkward middle child was also extremely shy and only wanted to work in the background setting up the chairs, tables and food. She chose to hang all the stars, using Mario as her ladder guard, to catch her if she fell. She would be the concierge for the event, showing guests to their seats and handing them their programs. Rico would be playing the sax, Bryen the cello, Frankie would recite something, Mario would do a magic routine; the oldest two were trying to come up with a skill that could be set to music or one that could be done without sending people into gut-clenching laughter. Then they decided that, yes that should be what they did, tell jokes and perform a comedy routine in order to send people into gut-wrenching laughter. Frank cracked up just hearing about the plans. While the children did their jobs,

Carmen and Maria spent lots of time alone in the pool during the days, relaxing and getting even more golden brown than each of their already pretty shades were.

The night for the production finally arrived and the Hazelton's and a few coworkers for each of the adults came out and proclaimed the event a total success. Each of the girls had a friend come and they loved it, praising Aubree for her producer's abilities. Her father told her to keep at it and later she might use it as a career and end up in Hollywood. Aubree was thrilled by the praise and promised to work hard and began planning for a fall production.

For the rest of the summer the family relaxed and waited for school to reopen. They felt that their home was like a resort, so they stayed home except for Drivers Education and appointments to the doctor for Carmen. The horses arrived and Frank had his friend from work come out to teach the boys how to care for them. The place began to look like a real farm; the family thrived and was happy. No one knew that Rico was just waiting until the day when he would become a man and could finally trump Bryen with Tawnie.

Chapter Thirteen

The years flew by and Carmen gave birth to two daughters and another son to add to the family of now thirteen. Over the next seven years, the kids stepped up their training in auto mechanics and over the road truck servicing. Doriano opened a shop on the property and Simon bred and trained horses to sale for rodeos and to farms. Rico graduated from high school in January of 75 and left for Juilliard early, wanting to have a head start on Tawnie. He wanted to be her guide around campus and the one she turned to when she got lonely because he did not think Bryen was good enough to get in to the highly prestigious school. It took discipline and a mind that was determined to succeed at what it set out to do, and that was Rico, but the act he was determined to carry out was not music related. He had his mind set on getting Tawnie by any means necessary.

Unbeknownst to either Tawnie or Bryen who remained chaste over the years, waiting until they could spend time together away at college, Rico pegged Bryen exactly on point. Bryen enjoyed the cello, but it was not his dream instrument. He did not have ulterior motives in learning how to play it, except to continue what he started because Tawnie came along and was encouraging to him. He received his letter during the winter of 75, because he and Tawnie were graduating early, in January 76. He did not get in, and was so disappointed that he cried on Tawnie's shoulder. She held him and said that she would not go, but it was a dream she'd had since he met her and he was not about to let her make that sacrifice for him, and neither was her father. He compromised and applied to NYU to be close to her. He got in, though not as happy he was satisfied and felt consternation not only toward himself but also toward his brother, who had been a pain in his ass since elementary school. He felt that Rico posed a threat to Tawnie and remembered the day that he first felt the unspecified way that Rico made him think that she was in trouble. Rico told his family that Tawnie would change her mind about which brother she was interested in, and even now the memory sent a hair-raising chill down Bryen's back. He would have to talk to her and try to make her understand the threat; not walk around feeling afraid, but to remain alert to the possible ways that Rico could hurt her.

Tawnie moved to New York and Juilliard and into the same dorm where Rico had his room. His parents and hers encouraged the two to remain close because they were oblivious to, but not apathetic toward any possible threats. They were parents, and had not heard about the real Rico. Bryen had, and believed it about his brother. While attending high school it was said that Rico was a "canine running around in heat" and several girls had claimed that he assaulted them, tearing one girls blouse off. She said she misinterpreted his actions and thought he wanted to kiss her and maybe touch her breasts. She said yes to that much, but no to taking things further. Rico called her a "cock tease", slapped her, and tore her blouse baring her breasts.

One of the other girls said Rico began their date as a nice person, buying her a sundae and taking her to the football game. Later that night when they returned to his car, he became Mr. Hyde. He asked her for oral sex, when she said no he forced her to perform it on him, choking her he was so huge, making her vomit. This angered him so much that he chased her down the street, calling her filthy names.

Bryen thought he would always be around to protect Tawnie, but now that she was at Juilliard without him, he would have to come up with a plan B. It would destroy his sweet girl if she had to go through what those other girls who confessed went through, because she had practically grown up around Rico. It would crush her to think that her judgment was flawed rather than understanding that Rico as a person was flawed. Was he always this way or had he inadvertently become someone other than who he used to be. Tawnie would probably blame herself if Rico did something to hurt her, wrongly suggesting that she somehow led him on rather than that he was a predator. Moreover, that is what happened.

Tawnie walked into her dorm room and said, "Wow, this is 'informally charming' meaning tacky." She knew it would only be for a few years and she could live with anything that long. What was going to be hard was trying to figure out what she wanted to do with her life after graduation. She thought she might want to go out to Hollywood and work with Aubree who was producing sitcoms. Well for now she was the assistant to the producer, but same thing to Aubree. Before she moved in any of her furniture or bedding, she went out and bought some paint and Rico and Bryen helped her paint her room. For two days she stayed with Bryen in his one bedroom apartment across town.

She loved the campus that was Juilliard and made sure that she was a part of everything that was going on. One hour she watched a play to see where it could be improved, another hour she helped a band put together a performance at one of the local cafes or clubs, and in the third hour, she listened while a single musician or singer worked on a piece of music or song in order to provide feedback. She felt like she had come to a third home at Juilliard. Her first home was her own, and Bryen's was her second home, and now Juilliard. Evidently, she was born listening to a lot of noise because wherever she was, it did not bother her.

Rico would often pick her up on his way to class and walk her to hers, so they became close. She would share whatever food she bought on the way from class in the evening, and he would take her out some evenings. They were in some of the same workshops and had to attend a concert soon. Tawnie thought it would save money for both of them to go together. Bryen couldn't go but asked her to take a friend along if she could. He strongly suggested it but didn't want to make her nervous or suspicious if there was no need to be. Tawnie told him, "Yes, Bry I've found a friend to go," so he stopped worrying and went away on his own class assignment.

At the last minute, the friend got sick with what looked like food poisoning. Tawnie went with Rico alone, unsuspectingly. They played beautifully, receiving standing ovations and curtain calls, and had flowers tossed onto the stage. It was a wonderful night and all the students received a personal invitation to attend a party afterwards. The alcohol flowed and everyone was drinking heavily. Rico promised to watch over Tawnie and not let her drink too much. Without paying attention to how much she was actually drinking, Tawnie got drunk, so drunk in fact that Rico carried her in his arms back to their hotel and took her to his room. He ran a hot bubble bath, eased her into it and with her incoherent raped her. Not just raped, for the whole night he ravished her, he treated her like a piece of raw meat and devoured her from head to toe. He started out stripping her out of her clothes and then put her into the bath water. He heard her moan but in his mind, she was telling him that it felt good to be there with him.   In reality, she said and thought nothing, she was totally out of it. He kissed her mouth, biting her plump lips, gnawing on them until they began to bleed. Seeing the blood fired his blood first to an increased heat level. Then he headed down her body licking and biting on her elongated nipples. Unconsciously her body responded to his manipulations of it, which any ones would have under the same circumstances. He sucked and bit on them, and his blood bubbled and then he went lower. He drained some of the water out so he could see every part of her vaginal area, and went to work on it. First with his mouth, doing everything he wanted to do to every other girl that he enticed to go out with him. He never got this far with any of them because he always moved to quickly, rushing into things instead of letting the female lead and easing into it. He showed his true colors too soon, sending warning signals and raising red flags. With Tawnie, because she met him and his brothers at such a vulnerable stage in her life, after being traumatized by her friend's death, she wanted to treat all other boys tenderly and compassionately, even if they showed a negative trait. She saw no negative traits in her friends, the Marichelli's. In fact, she trusted them all with her life.

Rico sucked on her clit, gnawing it forcing it in and out and Tawnie writhed under his stimulating assaults. She remained unconscious, no way consenting to this attack on her virginal body, a body that she was saving for Bryen. Rico's blood now boiled and he stroked his rock hard cock, leaking cum because of his excitement to finally have the one person he knew he would one day take possession of. He could not hold back any longer and shot his sperm all over her thighs, outside and in moaning out his pleasure. He began talking to Tawnie, "Aw baby, you liked that didn't you? I know you wanted me to take you, and finally we have our chance to be together. Oh yes, all night baby, and we've only just begun. Oh, yes music would be nice. I'll go put some on." Rico stepped out of the tub naked and went into the bedroom to find the jazz station on the radio. George Benson was playing his new hit, This Masquerade. Rico loved that album and so did Tawnie, so he turned it up thinking he heard her say do so. Now that he had Tawnie he could relax and have a few drinks, so he fixed himself a rum and coke. When he went back into the bathroom, he saw how uncomfortable Tawnie looked slumped in the tub, so he pulled her out, carrying her over his shoulder to the bed. Once she was laid out on the bed, he positioned her the way he always thought she would be on his bed, with raised knees and legs spread wide so he could see all of what he thought belonged to him. He used pillows to help prop her in just the right position. Talking again he said, "You look so sweet now, shall I dry you before we begin again. I hope you can participate more this time and not make me do all the work. Yes, Mr. Benson has such musicality. I know you love this but not as much as you love me, my darling girl. Oh yes, all night. No, no more to drink now precious and yes, I will taste you right now." He started in again, first by undoing her hair and rubbing his penis through it. Then he held both of her breasts together, squeezing them and placed his steel-like shaft between them and poured his drink over them as lubrication. He wasted no time but began thrusting his hips forward and back repeatedly until again he shot himself all over her mouth.

He got up and took a hot shower, wishing that he had not allowed her to get so drunk. He needed her so see at least some of what they were like together and how good it was for him. After drying off, he searched for something to eat and finding nothing called the front desk for room service. The connecting restaurant was still serving burgers and fries so ordered two burgers a fry and a bottle of rum, he was told he would have to show his identification to receive. He had plenty of fake ID's so that did not bother him. After eating and downing another rum and coke, he stretched out next to Tawnie on the bed. He began this round by suckling her breasts, nipping and gnawing the nipples while trying to avoid the area that he had bitten earlier, though it no longer dripped blood. He took her hands and wrapped them around his cock and worked her hand under his, pulling at his scrotum sack and finally rammed his cock into Tawnie, using the previous cum still clinging to her thighs as lubrication. Since she was still a virgin, she was extremely tight and her vaginal walls gripped down on Rico like a vise. He plunged and pumped continually until sweat dripped over her stomach and he reveled in the slippery feel of her body. To him she was agreeable to everything he was doing, having given her consent when she went to the concert with him in the first place. Nothing could have stopped him at this point; after all, he thought he was in the right. His ego and manipulative nature, all wrapped up in mental illness had driven him beyond a mere no. In fact no one had ever told him NO, that he could remember. He usually got his way, one way or another. He talked to a still unconscious Tawnie, asking her, "Are you tired yet baby. I think I'm about done for tonight if that's alright with you. We can bathe together in the morning. Yes, I love you too; and you're so welcome. I loved it too. Night night." He kissed her lips, trying to avoid the area that was turning purple and swollen. He turned away from her and went to sleep.

The next morning, Tawnie woke up sick and hurting with a headache that made her feel like someone had battered her brains out. She was cold, partially wet and was shivering. She had no idea where she was or why every part of her hurt. She began crying, deep wrenching sobs that woke Rico. When Rico turned to her, she was stunned that he was with her on a bed. "Rico where are we?"

"We're still in the hotel baby. You were drinking a little and we came back here. You wanted to have our own party, and of course, I wasn't going to turn you down. We had a bath, ate a little and I had a couple drinks to try to catch up to you. Are you feeling okay? You look a little worse for wear, but not too bad," he told her smirking.

"I feel sick, I hurt all over and I need to get to the bathroom to throw up but I need your help," she told him gasping through the tears.

"It's okay baby, I'm right here for you. I'll carry you, just wrap your arms around me. It's gonna be alright now. We had such a good time last night, didn't we?"

"Rico, honestly I don't remember a thing, sorry. If you say I had a good time and that I initiated this by telling you I wanted to start something with you, I can only say I'm glad you were with me and took care of me. Right now, I just want to sit on the toilet and then take a bath. I feel sticky, cold and can't stop shivering. Once I get myself together, can we just go?"

"Of course my love, anything you want I am willing to do. I'll leave you now, but I'm right out here. I'll call the school and cancel our classes for a few days using the flu as our excuse so take your time. We might as well plan to stay at least another night; we've missed check out time so it's paid for," he told her leaning in and kissing her near her lips.

"Thank you Rico." Rico shut the bathroom door leaving Tawnie alone and she broke down in wracking sobs, holding her arms around herself and trying to stay quiet. She tried to think over last night and wondered how she could have let this happened. She knew she was no longer a virgin, because she felt pains in her vagina, all the way up into her uterus. She felt like she had been pummeled by a battering ram up there. Evidently, Rico's penis was humungous because if that wasn't what he used then it must have been a broom stick.

The castigation and blame began. Tawnie believed Rico when he said that she wanted him, and that he just bowed to servicing her, looking out for her wants and desires. She was heartbroken over her own duplicity because she had promised herself to Bryen since they were children, and now she had behaved like the commonest of sluts. How would she ever be able to face Bryen again? She wouldn't. She would dirty the air he breathed from her own wanton behavior. Bryen was pure, clean, and healthy and she was a rotten seductress, she now thought. She cried even harder over the loss of her one true love, over the regrets of one mistake. She regretted taking this trip, remembering that Bryen told her to take along a chaperone. The school told them not to go anywhere without proper supervision and what had she done, tempted Rico into taking her off alone to be seduced.

Tawnie got into the tub and soaked away all the pain from her physical body but she couldn't soak away the thoughts running through her mind. She was shattered mentally because all her dreams and plans were ruined. She thought that she had ruined not only her own life but also that of her best friend. She tried to remember if Rico mentioned whether or not they had used a condom because she was not on the pill. Her plans with Bryen were to marry right after they graduated.

They would return home and begin a family immediately, therefore cutting out the need for birth control. She had to know if they were protected from an unwanted pregnancy. "Rico I was a virgin. Did we use protection?" she called through the door.

Rico was listening to and singing along with Freddie Jackson's Rock with me, on the radio, imaging that this could be their theme song for their lives together after last night. He planned to marry Tawnie and return home with her; now that he had her, his plans were complete. After the song ended Tawnie called again to Rico saying, "Rico, please come to the door. Did we use protection last night?"

"No, I saw no need to. If we get pregnant, we'll return home and get married. Isn't that what you want?"

"I would want it now, but it wasn't in my plan to get pregnant until after graduation. Bryen and I . . ."

"There is no more 'Bryen and I' for you Tawnie!" he shouted bursting through the bathroom door. "There's only you and me in the equation for our lives, baby! You made that choice! Now you have to live with it because I will not have my brother as a third in our bed! Can you understand that?" he ranted.

Tawnie was struck dumb; never having seen nor heard Rico raise his voice since they were little, she could not believe what she was hearing. Did Rico want her that much that he would shut Bryen out of their lives completely? Would she be able to explain that she had over indulged one night and now regretted it?

"Rico, what are you saying? You expect me to change all my plans because of this one mistake. We don't know that I'll even get pregnant. You can walk away and forget this ever happened. Don't you want that?"

"No! I-want-you! I've always wanted you! You are mine because you chose me, and that to me means forever! You're mine and I'll never let you go! Never! Now is it plain enough for you?" he shouted in her face, grabbing her hair and pulling her head back.

"Yes, Rico. Please calm down. I'm yours because I chose you. I'll be out in a minute."

"As a matter of fact, I think I'll stay in here with you and help you with your bath. Move to the front, so I can get in." Rico removed the towel he'd been wearing since they woke up. Tawnie looked between his legs and then understood why she was in such pain inside. He *had* used a battering ram, and there was the proof. He hung down like an engorged stallion. Is that what she would have to endure for the rest of her life? Good thing she was out of it when he took her the first time, she would have probably run, she thought.

Over the next hour, Rico showed Tawnie what she had missed last night but what she had to look forward to during their lives together. He took her in every way that he had ever heard of or read. He began slowly and tenderly, having calmed down. Tawnie had that effect on men; the ability to talk them around, calming them from their hysteria and it's good that she had that ability because with Rico she would need it. Even if she never gave him cause to berate her, he would do so over what he imagined to be slights and rejections from her. He kissed her from head to toe, licking and sucking her ears, eyes, nose and mouth. He moved down to her breasts, turning her around to face him, putting her thighs over his so she could ride him. He suckled at her breasts claiming them, saying, "These are mine Tawnie. Let me hear you say that these will always be mine."

Tawnie was ready to play the game in order to keep him calm. Now that she had made her bed so to speak, she would have to lie in it. That thought filtered through her mind and she heard her mother's voice saying it, 'If you put yourself in a position with a boy that you thought you wanted, and it turns out it was lust, it might come back to bite you in the butt. Then you would have made your bed, so you'll have to lie in it,' she'd said years ago. Her parents always preached to them about being chaste until marriage and being careful with bad associates. Tawnie couldn't let them think that she had made a mistake or that she ever regretted being with Rico. She wouldn't be able to face any one if she thought they pitied her and her decision. She would mourn the loss of Bryen but maybe he was only her schoolgirl crush and now that she was an adult, Rico was her adult choice. She prayed that it was so.

"These breasts, this body are all for you Rico and will always be for you." She leaned in and wrapped her arms around him, running her fingers through his hair, pulling at its length and massaging his scalp. He groaned deep in his throat but kept the beast hidden. He wondered if he could let the beast go, now that Tawnie was his. He smiled at her and pulled her close, positioning his cock at the opening to her hairy nest, and gave her a washcloth to bite down on. He rubbed his length before plunging inside her. She screamed in pain and shock, but remained still allowing Rico to lead her. He kept still too, allowing her passage to adjust to his preternatural length and girth. He knew he was more than the average man in that area and was proud of his size. He knew that Tawnie would come to love it, and he would help her get use to what it could do because he had plans to take her several times a day until she did.

"Tawnie, it might take some time getting used to my size, but with practice and patience we will become the greatest of lovers and last night was just a precursor. It was so good girl, and I'm sorry you missed it. But no worries, I will make love to you several times a day and most of the nights. We will soon know each other inside and out. Isn't that what you wanted when you told me to take your virginity, that you were tired of holding onto it?"

"Yes, Bry . . ." she began and before she knew it, Rico had backhanded her across the face.

"Never call me that name again! Do you understand?" he demanded and began driving himself into her sore tight passage. He bit down on her shoulder, on both sides of her neck and started to bite her ear, before she stopped him screaming, "Rico stop you're hurting me!" and began crying again. He remembered he had to recall the beast and put it back in restraints.

"Shhh, baby, I'm sorry, so sorry. Rub your hands through my hair again, and hold me close to your body. I can calm down. See, I'm calmer, you already know how to keep me calm baby."

"Yes, Rico. I can help you. We can help each other," and she started sucking his mouth, drawing out his tongue. He was training her well, and she would need to learn quickly in order to avoid being slapped and yelled. She now understood that Rico was damaged. He was unstable and in order to save herself, she would need to constantly give him reassure and give him as much time, attention and loving that she could possibly give. He was like a hungry infant crying out to be fed, with a mother that was too busy to take time for him.

Tawnie let him ride her and she did begin to feel some pleasure from his loving, though mostly pain for now. She knew it would get better, and she would do whatever it took to save herself. Keith Washington began to sing his latest, Kissing You on the radio, and Tawnie let herself go and moved with the music, into a false world, pretending that everything she was hearing was her very own life. She knew she could endure this, her new life if she could just keep up the pretense and not think about all she was losing.

Chapter Fourteen

Before Bryen could get to her and stop her from making the mistake of her life, Tawnie and Rico went to the NYC courthouse and got married. They stayed at Juilliard and waited to see if they were expecting. Rico went to the housing coordinator and asked to be put in married housing off campus. Several weeks later, they were able to move into an apartment off campus, and Tawnie intentionally did not contact Bryen to let him know. He had not heard from her in weeks and began hanging out around her classrooms. Every time she came out of class she was holding Rico's hand, and Bryen would slip away, not wanting a confrontation with Rico on campus. He knew it would be bad, because he could see that Rico was even crazier than he was as a youngster. Bryen never told anyone the scary things Rico had done and said during the times he and Rico had shared a room. He did not want to burst anyone's bubble; the bubble around the perception of them as a perfect family. That was before Carmen and Doriano came. After they moved in, he really kept his mouth shut; and Rico got worse.

Rico used to hide food; not his food from dinner, but other items from the kitchen cabinets. One day Bryen found several pieces of bread in Rico's sock drawer. The bread was old, moldy and crumbled when Bryen took it out to throw it away. On other occasions, he found a jar of peanut butter, a package of crackers, packs of coffee. Items that did not make any since to Bryen were in Rico's possession. As they grew up Bryen found dead rodents among Rico's belongings. He even found a squirrel once in a trunk that Rico had claimed from their grandfather's house. Bryen never found out whether Rico did something to the squirrel or if it was from their grandfather's time. All Bryen knew was that Rico needed watching and no one should ever make him angry.

Bryen dropped out of the current semester at NYU in order to try to catch Tawnie alone. One day after tracking their movements for several months, he saw Tawnie coming out of the building where she had most of her classes. Bryen knew that his was his chance to find out from her what was going on. He even wore a disguise so that she would not run away from him, knowing that she would not want to cross Rico. On this day he was dressed as a mailman, wearing the entire outfit and strolled causally up to her with what looked like mail in his hands and said, "My darling girl, don't run away or even act like you know who I am just in case Rico Is watching. Pretend I'm asking you to come down to the post office to pick up a package and follow me. Don't look around."

"Bry, what are you doing?" she asked him in a panicky voice, but followed him.

He led her around to the main building where the Administrative offices were, and into an empty conference room. When they got inside, he pulled her into his arms and said, "Tawnie, Tawnie, my love. What have you done to yourself getting mixed up with my brother?" She clung to him and began to cry, but he held her tight and began kissing her face, her neck and to kiss away her tears.

"Oh Bry, I didn't know, didn't even suspect what he had become. I'm scared that anything I might do would set him on a course of murder; either you or I could lose our life. Hold me tighter. What can I do? I think he got me drunk at the concert after party, or put something in one of my drinks while we were there. When I woke up, I was in the bed with him, naked and no longer a virgin. I think he raped me, and Bry, what leads me to that conclusion is that my body was ravished! I was bitten all over, Bry, even on the inside of my thighs near my pubic area. I was sore, sick and vomiting. The pain in my head and over my whole body makes me think that the drug didn't agree with my system. It took quite a few days before I felt like myself. Well as long as I'm with him, I'll never be myself again."

"Shh shh baby, don't cry, I'll figure something out. The only reason I haven't made a move yet is because I needed to know how you felt; wait for an opportunity to see the texture of your relationship, to see how deep it is. I had to know if you cared for him even a little, because if you had cared I would have left you alone with him and walked away. I didn't believe though that you could have been so superficial to forget what we've meant to each other all these years, baby. I couldn't find out without getting you alone. Tawnie he's sick, and he has planned this all along, setting traps for years, waiting like a black widow spider that seduces her mate, or a savage lion quietly hiding in the bush to snare its prey."

"Oh Bry, how could I have misjudged him? It's my fault!"

"Stop it Tawnie! I knew; my god I predicted you would do this! Start blaming yourself for the sins of my sick brother. He's left a stench of rottenness from here to Illinois. Nothing you did or didn't do caused any of this. This goes bone deep. It's genetic, an illness dating back to times innumerable. You know what they say, 'the sins of the father will be visited upon the next generation'. Who knows where exactly or with whom it began? I saw signs early on, but I was only a child and didn't want to make waves or cause friction that might break up the family. You saw us; we were on the verge of losing everything. Had my mom made one false move or made the wrong choice, my dad would have walked out and never looked back. I kept my mouth shut, and now look. So don't take this on yourself, and neither will I. We have to figure out what to do from this point forward. How long do you have, and where is he?"

"He went to an interview. I have two more classes, and he was meeting me after the second one, so I can stay with you for this class hour and part of the next, but I have to be either waiting at the classroom door, or out front when it's over."

"Good. Let's sit down on that sofa. I want to hold you for awhile; you're still shaking."

"Bry, I haven't stopped shaking since the morning I woke up with him laying next to me and I realized what had happened to me. It took me a few weeks to understand that I didn't ask for what he gave me; himself sexually."

"Don't try and clean the word up for that scum, call it what it was, rape! He raped you, probably repeatedly while you were under the influence of that date rape drug. Yes, I've heard about it being used on campuses around the country."

"Oh, Bry!," she gasped out. "What do I do, I'm carrying his child?"

"Yeah, I know. I see the bulge under the layers of clothing you wear to hide it. You can't hide anything from me though, I know your body like my own. We have never had intercourse but we've done everything else, and so I know every crease and crevice of you my love. It's too late to get an abortion, and . . ."

"Bry, this is your flesh and blood too, though its father may be sick it won't be! How can you even suggest I get rid of . . ."

"Tawnie, calm down. I wasn't suggesting it, I just made a statement of fact. If you don't want the child we could adopt it out, but, I was going to say since it is my blood I would love it because it grew and sheltered in your precious body, and your body has always in the past belonged to me. Does your body still belong to me and you, my sweet girl?"

"To answer your question, I will do this . . ." and Tawnie opened up her blouse, took out her breasts, and put Bryen's hands on them. She squeezed them, moaning and writhed holding onto his hands under hers and rubbed then down over her body. She leaned into him, kissing his lips, sucking on his neck, and guided his head down so he could suck from her breasts. He moaned, pulled her hand down to his cock, took it out, helped her rub him to his release and he shot his cum up in the air over her lap."

"Sorry, I was on a hair trigger edge and needed you so badly. Thank you for that. When can I see you, to be with you fully Tawnie as we planned?"

"Oh Bry. I'm not sure. I know there won't be many chances like this one. What costume shall I look for next time? You scared me to death this time. What I can do is give you our address and phone number. Then you can watch for me as you did today and if you see him leave, come up to our apartment. But Bry, I need you to work on a plan for something long term. I can't live like this, putting my baby at risk. For now, he hits me only in the face but who knows what he will do when we have a screaming infant around the house. Rico can't stand for my attention to be diverted away from him."

"I know all about him, and I am sweetheart, don't you worry about that. I don't want you involved just in case something goes wrong. I'll deal with Rico, you have my word on that and know it's been a long time coming." He kissed her long and deep, brushing his thumbs along her velvety soft, smooth jaw line. "I will only call if I see him leave, and I'll call to ask how long he'll be gone. I'll come wearing a utility workers uniform, okay?" He eased her up saying, "Try not to stress and don't do anything to set him off if you can help it, thought it doesn't take much I know. I think that now that he has you he's even more on edge because he knows that I will come for him soon."

"Baby, I'll try not to. I trust you as much as I love you. Are you working; how are you eating?"

"I give music lessons at the college if you can believe that. One of my professors has me working with him as a teacher's assistant and all my meals are included in the position. Don't worry about me. Just make sure this baby is safe until I can take you home," and he bent down and kissed her belly.

She held on to him trying to push through to his insides she was so unhappy without him. He rubbed her back, kissed her forehead and turned her toward the door. "You better go otherwise you'll be late and we don't want that. You have my numbers, but keep them in a safe place, maybe your shoes. Call me when you feel it necessary. I love you just as much as I always have, and nothing has changed for me, okay?"

"Okay." Tears were leaking from her eyes as she turned and walked away. Bryen felt desolated at the sight and knew that once he took care of their problem, he would never watch her walk away from him again.

Chapter Fifteen

Tawnie lay in her bed looking at the ceiling and reviewing her meeting with Bryen. She felt relieved that he was still around to love her and to help her. No way could she tell her parents or his parents what Rico had done to her. All they knew was that she had changed her mind; was now married to Rico instead of Bryen. Maybe one day she would be able to tell parts of the truth but never all of it. It was just to sickening to know. She had almost allowed herself to sink in to a deep depression over Rico's mental health issues. Instead, she gave herself permission to climb back out, stand strong and be patient; knowing that with a strong man like Bryen supporting her, she could defeat the monster who had taken over her life, her husband. She rubbed her baby bump and sang one of her favorite songs ' You' by Jesse Powell. It would become her anthem while she stayed with Rico, all the while thinking of Bryen when she sang.

She wondered what it was Bryen had in mind to relieve them of this situation. She just hoped it would end soon, because every time she heard Rico come into the apartment she began to feel sick to her stomach. At her last doctor's appointment, the nurse reported that her blood pressure was high and in order to avoid a possible stroke while pregnant she would need to avoid all stressful situations. Tawnie wanted to laugh in her face and ask how, when it was her beloved husband who was the cause of it. He was sitting right there with her so she could not say what she was thinking. The nurse told her to try to get as much rest as possible, lying in a dark cool room alone. She evidently saw the bruises on her body and knew that it was her husband causing her problems. Rico had eased up on hitting her because the doctor told him that it was dangerous for a pregnant woman to get any kind of bruise; that it could lead to blood clotting which might travel to her lungs and kill her and the baby. Evidently, Rico wanted the baby more than he cared about hurting Tawnie, and tonight she planned to talk to him to find out why.

After she served him potatoes and pot roast, using Maria's recipe, she asked Rico if he would rub her back because she was feeling pains that might lead to pre-term labor, and she saw the fear in Rico's eyes. Now would be a good time to talk about it she thought and asked, "Rico, how do you feel about me getting pregnant so soon into this relationship? We never even had a honeymoon?"

"I wanted this more than anything else Tawnie. You remember that song by Bobby Womack, If you think you're lonely now? He starts out by saying 'everybody needs somebody to love', and 'if you think you're lonely now wait until tonight girl' well thats the theme song to my life. Who did I ever have to love me?"

"Don't you know that you're parents loved you Rico? Parents always love their children, no matter how many they have. Each child is loved, though they are loved in a different way. Are you telling me you never felt loved by either of your parents?"

"Not for myself, no. I never felt love from either of them the way a child is supposed to feel love. I don't remember hearing I love you Rico, only 'you kids know we love you.' Our child that you carry will have to love me as its parent, love me because I gave it life. I've wanted you from the beginning Tawnie."

"What beginning Rico?"

"From the time you moved into our neighborhood. We were out shooting baskets and we saw you get out of the truck. Bryen said something about the way you looked and then I saw you and knew I wanted you for myself."

"Rico, is it possible you wanted me because you heard Bryen say it first? Were you just trying to best him as you were trying to best him in sports? When a man loves a woman, he can't keep his mind on anything but her. Is that how you feel about me today? Would you give up all your comforts for me, and do me no harm even if you do get angry with other people or things. You should hold me dear to your heart and never allow anyone or thing to harm me. Is that how you feel about me Rico? Think about it and tell me the answer in the morning, okay?"

She looked over at him and he was sound asleep. Damn! She thought that tonight she might have gotten some answers as to what makes him tick. I have to get him in to see a professional. He'd never agree to it willingly she knew because he could never admit to having a problem; the sick never do. Her baby's life would be at risk and that she could not allow, would fight like a mother bear with her cub to protect her child.

She returned to her thoughts about Bryen, and remembered his scent, his touch and his appearance. Over the year's he had grown tall and now stood six feet to her five foot two inches. He still looked like Gregory Peck, even more so now that he had grown up and the hour she had spent with him reminded her how much they loved each other, and longed to be together. Oh how she wished it were he here on the bed with her instead of this stranger who she was married to. One day, he'd promised her and she believed him. It wasn't Rico she had planned her life with, and he admitted he wanted her only because Bryen saw her first. For Rico everything boiled down to a competition between him and his brothers. She would not be his prize; she'd already been won.

Bryen was not idle but busy setting up a plan to bring down Rico and make him pay for the damage he had done to several of the girls who he met in high school. When Bryen heard what he had done to Tawnie, he left her and got sick to his stomach. He called the FBI and had them get affidavits from the girls who Rico assaulted. They were anxious to have the matter resolved and were willing to go to court and testify against him. The FBI put a plant or a mole in Juilliard to get close to Rico; a beautiful female who was pretending to be a student that played the trumpet. The female agent had made successful contact with Rico, and she had already been out with him. The plan was to set up a concert away from New York so that Rico would have to be away from Tawnie over night. He would be booked in a hotel and the plan was to catch him trying the same things he had done previously, but this time on someone who was knowledgeable about his treacherous nature, had the backing of law enforcement and was ready for him. Bryen wanted the trap to snap shut on the hunter this time and not the prey.

A week later while watching their apartment, Bryen saw Rico leave so he called Tawnie and she said he had a class but that her feet were swollen causing her to stay home. Bryen went up to spend the hour with her. He knew that he could make her feel better by giving her sympathy and rubbing her feet. He would tell her of the plans for Rico's take down and capture. He wanted to make sure she would not be going on the trip, and would not be in harm's way. When Rico found out he had been set up Bryen knew his beast would rage and someone could get killed. Bryen had purchased an Italian Baretta 92 and kept it cocked and loaded at all times. He did not trust that Rico had not gone out and got a gun himself, so he wanted to be a step ahead of him or at least on the same step. If he felt threatened or thought Tawnie was ever again put in harm's way, he wouldn't hesitate to drop him. What Tawnie and hopefully Rico did not know was that Bryen had moved into the same building, just around the corner from them, on the same floor. If he so much as heard a peep of anger, he was going to bust down their door and take Rico out. He was tired of his shenanigans.

Bryen wrapped Tawnie in a cashmere robe that he brought over as a gift for her, sat her next to him on the couch with her feet in his lap and rubbed them. He wanted to take things into the bedroom but he didn't want to do anything in his brother's home; that wasn't his style, but Rico's. Their time would come and he could wait, showing patience for his secret lover. As he rubbed her feet and ankles, they talked about their lives and listened to The Dramatics on the stereo singing their latest release 'In the Rain'. "How are the little ones back home at your house Bryen?"

"Everyone is growing up and doing well. Francesca is seven and in second grade. She's just as beautiful as you would think. Giovanni is four and a terror, only controlled by dad and Shelby is two and a precious doll. Carmen stayed home and has an office that dad built on the side of the house for her practice. Mom is now working at Memorial hospital in the cardiac unit, and loving it. How is our little princess doing today, other than causing her mama's fell and ankles to swell?" he asked rubbing Tawnie's protruding belly.

"So, you're betting a girl huh? A daughter would be nice."

"I think a healthy baby would be a wonderful gift. The way our lives are going if we can just get it born, I'll be happy," Bryen told her sounding exhausted.

"Why do you sound so tired, Bryen?" she asked him. "I hope you're taking care of yourself? I know that was meant to be my job, to take care of you and I'm sorry I can't right now. Soon my love, soon," she told him, running her hands through his hair.

Chapter Sixteen

Over the next few weeks, Bryen stayed in close contact with the parties involved in the takedown of Rico. He would be charged with federal crimes because unbeknownst to him, he had crossed into another state when he drove one of the young women out in the country and assaulted her. In addition, what he had done to Tawnie was now a federal crime because she was a student of a college that received federal monies and was under the supervision of federally paid staff. The case was building into more than anyone expected it would be. The feds said Rico might have rushed to marry Tawnie so that she could not testify against him. What he didn't know was that his theory was flawed because a new law passed that year in New York State stated, 'crimes committed against a female by her spouse if drugs were in any way involved would be prosecuted to the fullest extent of the law using her testimony against him'. They had him on multiple federal charges and the trap slammed shut.

The concert was set up, tickets purchased and the hotel bill paid for in advance by the feds. Bryen planned to move Tawnie into his apartment after the arrest so that she could continue her education, have her baby and both of them graduate. He wanted all of their plans to succeed.

The night Rico left for the event, Bryen slipped into the apartment and sat with Tawnie. Together they waited to hear from the feds that everything took place as they assumed it would with the information they had about Rico's predatory nature and his history. The call that came was not exactly what they wanted to hear. Rico did just as they knew he would; going after the agent, slipping a drug in her drink, which was caught on tape. He took her up to his room, assaulted her but before they could break in he had cut her face with a broken shard of glass. His beast had burst forth in a rage so fierce that he broke out of the grip of the rescuing agents and got away. He got as far as the hotel lobby, turned on the agents with his own weapon and they ended up shooting him down. His last words were, "Tell Tawnie the baby . . ." and then he died. He was DOA at the hospital.

Bryen held Tawnie as she cried, her body shaking with wracking sobs that he knew would raise her blood pressure putting her and the baby at risk. He caressed her mumbling soothing words of love to try to get through to her. He knew she was blaming herself for all that had happened. All he could do was be there, try and give her comfort, but he knew that she loved Rico in her own way. She would not have been able to live with him and not feel some kind of deep connection with him. They had made love on numerous occasions, she carried his child and that was okay with Bryen. He would mourn the potential of his brother, what he could have been had he not been born with or was influenced by the particular flaw that eventually led to his death. Bryen would have to stay strong for not only Tawnie, but for all the members of their family and the friends that thought they knew Rico. He and Tawnie would try and never disclose the true nature of what he was, leaving the family a picture of innocence to mourn and bury.

After the funeral, Bryen and Tawnie continued with their education and over the next four years delivered a son, found teaching assignments and planned to move back home to plan a wedding and be close to family and loved ones.

On her wedding day, Tawnie woke up nauseous and knew exactly what it meant. She waited to tell Bryen that they were expecting a baby in the next year, because she wanted his mind to remain clear. Just getting though this event would be enough to rattle any man's nerves. Her gown was a strapless empire waist cream colored confection and she looked like the bride on top of a cake. She wore diamond drops in her ears given to the sisters from their paternal grandmother and a pearl necklace from their maternal grandmother. Both pieces had been given to them by their husbands and would be passed around to all the sisters to wear on their individual wedding day.

As she walked down the aisle she heard a compellation of music from Stevie Wonder and The Temptations, but their first dance was to The Jacksons's 'Lovely One'. They all danced until the wee hours of the morning to music the family chose for the band to play and had a wonderful celebration.

Over the next few years all the sisters married, had a child each and bought homes out near The Marichelli Manor as it was later named. Tawnie and Bryen remained friends first and then lovers, never allowing anything or anyone to come between them.

The End

About The Author

Thanks for reading Cry for Me and please leave a review.

If you have not read my other books, please consider doing so. There are four digitals books in the Mississippi Plantation series: Chained to Love. The darker side of Slavery, book one. Run for your Life! MaDea's Story, book two. The Callendar Sisters, Mail-Order Brides, book three. MaDea's Plantation Cookbook. Recipes from the Old South, book four. If you'd rather have paperback, the books are all compiled into one book, under the title Chained to Love, also. And MaDea's cookbook is in paperback format, too. My newest release is Her Master, His Slave! Please look for it at CreateSpace.com.

Toni.

Made in the USA
Columbia, SC
11 July 2017